The

Sunshine State Cookbook

George S. Fichter

Illustrated by
Alexa Jaffurs

Pineapple Press, Inc.
Sarasota, Florida

Inquiries should be addressed to:

Pineapple Press, Inc.
P.O. Box 3889
Sarasota, Florida 34230

www.pineapplepress.com

Library of Congress Cataloging in Publication Data

Fichter, George S.
      The Sunshine State cookbook / [George S. Fichter].—1st ed.
          p.   cm.
      Includes index.
      ISBN 1-56164-214-2
      1. Cookery—Florida. I. Title.

TX715.F43 2000
641.59759—dc21

                                    00-061136

First Edition
10 9 8 7 6 5 4 3

Cover photo by Cynthia Thuma
Book design by *osprey*design
Printed in the United States of America

CONTENTS

Introduction vi

Fruits and Desserts 3

Fish and Shellfish 75

Vegetables 127

Meats and Poultry 197

Index 207

INTRODUCTION

FLORIDA is a cornucopia of foods—both the ordinary and the extraordinary. Here you can find not only the fruits, vegetables, fish, and meats of temperate climates but also those of the subtropics. Florida is the winter vegetable basket for much of North America, supplying tomatoes, potatoes, celery, beans, and many others for northern markets and with ample supplies for local consumption. But in Florida markets there are also cassavas, malangas, boniatos, chayotes, calabazas, mangoes, sapodillas, and other fruits and vegetables that are at first unfamiliar to Florida newcomers. With exceptions, their peak season is summer. More exotics are yard-grown and never go to market but are relished by those who make their acquaintance.

So this is a specialty cookbook. It is not complete—but no cookbook ever is. The recipes continue to change as they are used. And this one has a double purpose: to help both visitors and residents find new and exciting ways to use long-familiar foods and also to introduce them to new taste treats. *The Sunshine State Cookbook* is an updated version of an earlier book of Florida cookery, with new recipes and a sharper focus on the state. Enjoy!

George S. Fichter

1.

Fruits & Desserts

Florida and the nearby islands of the subtropics provide residents and visitors with a variety of fruits entirely different from those of temperate regions. Many are available fresh at the markets and in an increasing abundance to satisfy the demands of people who have either visited places where the fruits grow or who once lived there and have now moved to Florida. Some of the rare kinds can be obtained only if you grow them yourself or get acquainted with someone who does and who has ample surplus for sale or to give away. Don't expect these fruits to taste exactly like the kinds you know from temperate regions. They are different and distinctive. You may discover some that, to you, are far better than any fruit you have ever eaten. Others you may not like at first, but if you try them several times and in different ways, you may acquire such a taste for them that they will rank among your favorites.

COCONUTS

This familiar fruit is from a palm tree that is sometimes called "man's most useful tree." In tropical regions, the broad fronds are used in thatching houses. The roots are sometimes pulverized to make a coffee-like drink, and the sap of the tree is converted into palm wine. Unripened fruit provides a refreshing, clear drink that is kept surprisingly cool inside its heavily insulated container. The hollowed-out nuts make good containers or ornaments, and the

Incidentally, young or immature coconuts make an excellent dessert themselves. Simply cut them open and spoon out the soft meat. They are best if chilled first.

fibers of the husks are woven into mats. The meat of mature nuts is tender and sweet, and it can be eaten raw or cooked. Coconut oil is expressed or cooked from this meat.

Though a disease wiped out many of south Florida's coconut palms, at this writing the government is making an effort to reestablish coconuts in Florida. They are still available in markets. Coconuts are not utilized fresh in great quantity mostly because of the difficulty of husking them. Cutting into an already husked coconut is, of course, simple. To get the fluid out first—and never buy a coconut that does not have liquid "sloshing" inside—find the three dark "eyes" on the outside. Pierce at least two of these soft spots with an ice pick or some similar instrument, then pour the liquid from one of the holes; the other will let air inside to replace the liquid and keep it following smoothly. The shell can then be tapped with a hammer. It will break apart easily so that the meat can be cut out.

The uses of fresh coconut are numerous. Only a few are given here, but once you begin using fresh coconut, you will probably prefer it to the packaged or canned product. For one thing, there is a great satisfaction of knowing that you got the coconut yourself.

Coconut milk is obtained by grating coconut and then pouring warm water over it. This mass can then be pressed or placed in a loosely woven bag and squeezed. The solid portion is discarded. The whitish milk is used for cooking. (E.g., See Coconut Sherbet, next page.)

Coconut Pudding

    1 coconut, the meat grated
    1 pint milk
    ½ lb. sugar
    1 tsp. lime juice
    4 eggs
    ¼ lb. bread crumbs

Separate egg yolks from white. Beat the yolks, then stir in the lime juice, sugar (save out 2 tbsp. sugar), and milk. Add the coconut and bread crumbs, mixing thoroughly. Pour into a greased baking dish and place in oven at 325 degrees for about 20 minutes. Remove from oven and top with a meringue made by beating egg whites until they are stiff, then adding sugar and continuing to beat until the mixture stands stiffly. Cover the pudding with the meringue and brown the top in oven before serving. Serves 3-4.

For a variation, add a few drops of vanilla and about ¼ tsp. nutmeg to coconut and bread crumb mixture before stirring.

Toasted Coconut Bread Fingers

    1 ½ cups freshly shredded coconut
    1 cup sweet condensed milk
    8-10 slices of day-old bread

Trim crusts from bread and discard. Cut each slice into four strips. Dip these "fingers" one at a time into condensed milk and then into the shredded coconut. Make certain the slices are covered on both sides. Place fingers on greased cooky sheet and bake at 325 degrees for about 15 minutes or until they are browned. Remove from sheet and cool before serving. Serves 4-6.

Coconut Sherbet

    3 tbsp. freshly grated coconut
    1 pt coconut milk
    3 tbsp. water

½ lb. sugar
2 drops almond extract

Dissolve the sugar in water, heating slightly if necessary. Cool and then stir in the coconut milk. Add the almond extract and mix. Pour into tray and place in freezer. As soon as the mixture begins to be mushy, remove and beat until frothy. Return to freezer and allow to remain until well frozen. Serve with freshly grated coconut on top. Serves 4.

Coconut-Orange Salad (Ambrosia)

oranges, peeled and sliced
freshly grated coconut
sugar
lettuce

Arrange slices of oranges on lettuce leaves, using one orange per person to be served. Sprinkle the orange slices with sugar. Place a heap of freshly grated coconut in the center, about 1 tbsp. per serving. This can be eaten with no dressing or can be sprinkled with orange or lime juice and honey. Allowing the orange slices to marinate in orange or lime juice and honey in the refrigerator for a day before serving improves the flavor. Then remove and place on lettuce leaf as above.

Coconut and Sweet Potato Pudding

1 lb. sweet potatoes
1 coconut, the meat grated
juice from 2 limes
1 lb. sugar

Peel sweet potatoes, boil and mash. Mix in the sugar, coconut, and lime juice. Place in a greased baking dish at 375 degrees for about 45 minutes. Serves 4-6.

Coconut Dreams

2 coconuts, the meat grated

1 egg white, beaten
½ tsp. almond extract
4 cups sugar
1 tsp. vanilla extract

Set aside ½ cup of grated coconut. Combine remaining coconut with egg white and sugar in a saucepan, adding the "water" from inside the coconut or ¼ cup water if the coconut water has been discarded. Cook on a low heat until the mixture begins to thicken and becomes syrupy. Remove from heat and add the vanilla and almond extract, mixing. Drop this mixture by the spoonful onto waxed paper. Sprinkle with the grated coconut that was saved. Cool and eat. Serves 4-6.

Coconut Fritters

1 coconut, the meat shredded
¼ cup orange juice
½ tsp. grated orange rind
⅓ cup milk
1 egg, beaten
¼ tsp. salt
½ tsp. baking powder
1 cup flour, sifted
confectioners' sugar

Mix flour, baking powder, and salt in a bowl. Add egg, milk, orange juice, orange rind, and coconut. Mix thoroughly. Drop by the spoonful into deep fat at 375 degrees. Remove when golden brown and dry on absorbent paper toweling. Sprinkle with confectioners' or powdered sugar. Serves 4.

Coconut Cream Pie

1 large coconut, the meat grated (¾ to 1 cup needed)
3 egg yolks
2 cups milk
1 cup sugar
3 tbsp. cornstarch

¾ tsp. vanilla
⅛ tsp. salt
½ cup whipping cream
1 9-inch pie shell

Mix the sugar, cornstarch, and salt. Heat the milk to near boiling and add the dry ingredients slowly, stirring until the mixture is smooth. Cook in a double boiler, stirring frequently. Cool, then add the egg yolks and ⅓ of the coconut while the mixture is still lukewarm. Return it to the double boiler and cook until it thickens. Cool, stirring in the vanilla. Pour into pie shell. Whip the cream and spread it over the custard to the pie shell. Sprinkle remaining coconut over the top.

CERIMANS, OR MONSTERAS

This unusual fruit belongs to the same family as the malanga, described in the vegetable section of this book. No other member of the family produces edible fruit.

In Florida and throughout the tropics, these plants are commonly grown as ornamentals, for the sprawling vines produce a luxuriant growth of deeply lobed leaves that are as much as three feet long and two feet wide. The fruit, which appear during the summer rainy months, are about a foot long and as big around as an ear of corn, which they resemble. On its surface, each fruit consists of hexagonal plates that cover a creamy soft pulp that has a flavor like a banana and pineapple combined. The fruit must not be eaten until it is fully ripe, however, as until then it contains an abundance of calcium oxalate crystals that are irritatingly prickly to the tongue and inside of the mouth. Always make certain to remove the black outer covering over the pulp. When the fruit is fully ripe and ready to eat, the sections fall apart easily. If you have an abundance, mix them with chopped nuts and guavas or mangoes for a delicious fruit salad.

Cerimans or monsteras are only rarely seen in markets. People who know the fruit look forward eagerly to the ripening of their crop and consume it at home, but the plants are grown principally as ornamentals and only secondarily for their fruit. The real pity is that many people let the fruit go to waste without knowing how good it is.

PINEAPPLES

Long before the arrival of European explorers, the Indians living in Brazil were growing pineapples and had carried the fruit into other areas of the American tropics and subtropics. Columbus was the first European to taste this delicious fruit. Over the following two centuries, the pineapple was introduced to warm areas throughout the world. Now three-fourths of the pineapples grown commercially come from Hawaii.

Throughout the subtropics and in most of Florida, pineapples can be grown by home gardeners. Some are produced commercially. One of these fresh, mature pineapples ripened on the plant is unbelievably sweet and juicy, far superior to those that must be picked green and shipped long distances. A peculiarity of the pineapple compared to other fruits is that the stem passes completely through the fruit, forming a fibrous core that must be removed when the pineapple is prepared for eating. At the top of this stem—the upper end of the fruit—is a small rosette of leaves. If the top of the pineapple is sliced off and planted, it will grow, requiring about three years before it bears fruit. It will continue to produce fruit for several years, suckering new plants from its base.

In addition to being eaten fresh, the pineapple has numerous uses in salads and cooking. A few of these are suggested here.

Pineapple Delight

shredded pineapple
marshmallows
strawberry preserves
whipped cream

Place a layer of shredded pineapple in each dessert dish. Add two or three marshmallows that have been cut into small pieces. Cover with a layer of strawberry preserves and then another layer of pineapple, topping with whipped cream.

For variations, add shredded coconut or chopped nuts to the whipped cream.

Pineapple-Grapefruit-Strawberry Salad

1 cup finely diced pineapple
1 cup strawberries
1 grapefruit, sectioned

Mix the fruits and chill. For salads, drain and serve on a lettuce leaf. For a dessert, do not drain. Place the mixture in dessert dish and serve. A spoonful of honey can be added on top.

For a variation, if fresh Florida strawberries are not available, use canned cherries, peaches, or fruit cocktail. Celery and chopped nuts can also be added. Grapes, either alone or with other fruits, also combine nicely with pineapple.

Pineapples, too, can survive in conditions that are seemingly hostile to plants, but they produce the best fruits when well-fertilized and supplied with adequate moisture in well-drained soil.

Pineapple Sauce

2 cups finely diced pineapple
1 cup pineapple juice
1 tbsp. cornstarch
⅓ cup sugar
1 lime

Heat pineapple with pineapple juice and the juice from the lime. When mixture begins to boil, add cornstarch and sugar, which have already been combined. Stir constantly and continue cooking on medium heat until mixture thickens. Remove from heat and allow to cool. This can be used as a topping for ice cream, spread over ham or other meats, or eaten separately.

Pineapple Sherbet

1 ½ cups fresh pineapple, diced
1 lime
1 orange
1 pt. milk
½ lb. sugar

Save 2 tbsp. of diced pineapple. To the remainder of the pineapple, add the juice of the lime and ½ of the orange. Place in the refrigerator. Dissolve sugar in warmed milk and then also place in refrigerator to cool. As soon as both the milk and fruit are cold, mix the two and beat vigorously or place in a blender at low speed. Pour into tray and place in freezer. Remove when mixture is mushy and beat thoroughly one more time, then return to freezer. Serves 4.

Rummed Pineapple

1 pineapple
¼ cup sugar
¼ cup rum
1 tsp. cinnamon

Cut top from pineapple and save. Cut out the flesh of the pineapple, being careful not to pierce the outer shell. Throw away the core but save and dice the flesh. Also save the juice. Mix sugar with the fruit and replace in the hollowed-out shell. Pour in the pineapple juice and half of the rum, sprinkling cinnamon over the top. Fasten top on pineapple with heavy toothpicks. Place in oven at 375 degrees and bake until fruit is tender. Remove top and pour remaining rum over the whole pineapple. Light with a match to serve as a flaming dessert. Serves 3-4.

Pineapple Cheesecake

1 cup pineapple, finely diced or crushed
16 graham crackers
1 cup sugar
1 ½ lbs. cream cheese
4 eggs
1 tsp. vanilla
1 pt. sour cream

Crush graham crackers and place in bottom of an angelfood cake pan, tamping down firmly. Place crushed pineapple on top. Mix all of the remaining ingredients and pour over the pineapple. Bake at 350 degrees for one hour. Serves 4-6.

Stuffed Pineapple

1 pineapple
2 bananas
1 apple
2 peaches
1 pt. strawberries
2 oranges
sugar
whipped cream

Cut pineapple in half lengthwise and scoop out flesh, being careful not to break the outer shell. Discard the core but save and dice the flesh. Slice strawberries. Peel other fruits and cut into pieces.

Sprinkle with sugar and mix together. Place fruit in hollowed pineapple halves and top with whipped cream. Serves 3-4.

For a variation, soak the strawberries in a sweet wine for at least an hour before mixing with other fruits. Top with ice cream rather than whipped cream. Rum can be poured over the top.

The kinds of fruit can be varied or substitution made. Mango and papaya, for example are two excellent additions from the subtropics.

Pineapple-Nut Bread

   1 cup pineapple, diced or crushed
   1 cup chopped pecans or almonds
   ⅓ cup milk
   ⅓ cup salad oil
   4 tsp. baking powder
   ¾ tsp. salt
   1 egg
   3 cups flour

Break egg in mixing bowl and beat lightly. Add milk, nuts, pineapple, and salad oil, stirring thoroughly. Sift flour and baking powder, stirring in salt and sugar; add to ingredients in mixing bowl. Stir but do not beat. Place in bread pan and bake at 350 degrees for one hour. Serves 3-4.

Pineapple Omelet

   1 ½ cups fresh pineapple, diced
   6 eggs
   3 tbsp. milk
   2 slices of bacon, diced
   ¾ cups grated mild cheese
   ½ tsp. salt

Fry bacon on medium heat until crisp. Remove and place on absorbent paper towels. Pour bacon grease from skillet, leaving only about 1 tbsp.

Crack eggs into bowl. Separate yolks from whites and beat yolks lightly. Add salt, milk, crisp bacon, and cheese, mixing thoroughly. Beat egg whites until stiff, then fold into the yolk mixture. Pour into skillet and cook on low heat until omelet is browned on one side. Place in a pan in oven at about 250 degrees and leave until top is dried. Heat pineapple in its juice in saucepan until mixture begins to boil and thickens. Make cuts on each side of center of omelet and pour in pineapple mixture. Fold omelet and lift onto serving platter. Serves 4.

Pineapple-Ham Salad

1 cup fresh pineapple, finely diced
1 cup diced ham
1 egg, well beaten
butter
1 tbsp. prepared mustard
1 tbsp. pineapple juice
2 tbsp. milk

Mix ham, pineapple, mustard, and pineapple juice. Spread on slices of buttered bread and make sandwich. Add milk to egg and pour into small pie pan. Put each sandwich in pan. turning them over so that both sides are coated with mixture. Saute sandwiches in butter until browned on each side. Enough for 6-8 sandwiches.

BANANAS

To people from temperate regions, bananas are strictly a fruit—to be eaten out of hand or in some sort of dessert, generally simply prepared. Further, there is one kind of banana: the long, slim yellow commercial variety. It is surprising to these people to discover that there are literally dozens of kinds of bananas and that they have different flavors and uses. Some lend themselves best to baking. Others are used mainly as vegetables, as described in the vegetable section of this book. Among the kinds eaten without being cooked, there are types that have a distinct "ice cream" flavor and others that resemble pineapples, dates, apples, etc.

The banana "tree" is really a giant herb that has a treelike trunk. Some varieties grow as much as 25 feet tall, and the leaves may be 12 feet long. Bananas are grown commercially principally in Latin American, but there are numerous small plantings, usually for individual use, in southern Florida and the subtropical islands to the south. The plants are frequently incorporated in landscaping to add to the subtropical appearance. The bonus benefit is a harvest of homegrown fruit. Bananas grow and produce well only in moist, well-fertilized soil.

Banana Salad

1 banana for each person
finely chopped peanuts
maraschino cherries
lime juice
sugar
lettuce

Sweeten the lime juice with sugar. Roll bananas in the juice and then in crushed peanuts, coating surface of bananas with the nuts. Place banana on lettuce leaf and garnish with 1 or 2 maraschino cherries.

For a variation, use strawberries rather than maraschino cherries, or a combination of strawberries and white grapes.

Baked Bananas with Rum

6 bananas
½ cup brown sugar
3 tbsp. lime juice
1 tsp. allspice
¼ cup rum
butter

Cut peeled bananas in half lengthwise and place in a flat, greased baking pan. Sprinkle surface with brown sugar, then pour mixture of lime juice and rum over the top. Dot surface with butter. Add a small amount of water to pan—just enough to cover the bottom—and place in oven at 350 degrees for about 45 minutes. Turn bananas two or three times during the cooking period. Serves 6.

Quick Banana Ice Cream

1 qt. iced milk, vanilla
6 bananas
1 tbsp. lime juice

Combine all ingredients in electric blender and mix thoroughly at high speed. Place in freezing tray and refreeze. Can also be made by using 1 cup of orange juice instead of lime juice.

Banana Bread

4 large bananas, mashed
1 cup sugar
4 tbsp. butter of margarine
1 ½ cups flour
¼ tsp. salt
1 tsp. baking soda
2 eggs
1 cup chopped nuts (almonds, pecans, or mixed)

Mix all ingredients thoroughly and place in a greased bread pan. Bake at 375 degrees for an hour.

Spiced Bananas

6 bananas, peeled and cut crosswise into thirds
1 tbsp. lime juice
½ lb. brown sugar
1 tsp. nutmeg
1 tbsp. butter
1 tsp. cinnamon

1 tsp. grated orange peel
1 tbsp. chopped nuts
¼ tsp. powdered cloves or allspice for substitute
salt
1 cup cooking wine
4 coconut macaroons, crumbled or 3 tbsp. grated coconut

Moisten bananas with lime juice and fry in butter to which a dash of salt has been added. Heat wine, adding sugar and spices, and cook on low heat until it thickens. Put bananas on greased baking dish, and pour syrup over them, topping with the crumbled macaroons and nuts. Bake at 350 degrees for 20 minutes or until top is browned. Serves 4-6.

Banana Spread

4 ripe bananas
½ tsp. salt
1 tbsp. butter
1 ½ tbsp. sugar
1 ½ tsp. lime juice
8 slices lightly toasted bread

Mash bananas and mix them with the sugar, lime juice, salt, and butter. Spread on slices of bread and place in oven at 400 degrees for about 5 minutes. Serves 4-6.

Flaming Rummed Bananas

6 bananas, peeled and cut in halves, lengthwise
½ pt. rum
¼ lb. brown sugar
1 tbsp. butter, melted
milk

Mix sugar and butter with enough milk to blend them thoroughly, then place in a saucepan and bring to a boil. Remove from heat and cool. Put bananas in casserole and cook at 350 degrees for 10 minutes. Remove and pour over them half of the rum and all of the sugar–butter–milk mixture, which has been reheated. Return to oven for 5 minutes. Remove and pour remaining rum over the top. Light with a match as it is served. Serves 4-6.

Baked Bananas

1 banana per person, firm or slightly green
butter or margarine

Peel bananas and brush with softened butter or margarine. Place in a buttered baking dish and bake at 375 degrees for about 15 minutes or until tender.

Banana Tart

6 bananas
¾ cup sugar
2 tbsp. butter
1 lime, juice of
⅛ tsp. salt
½ tsp. nutmeg
whipped cream
pie shell (8 or 9 inch)
¼ cup white wine

Peel bananas and mash thoroughly. Place in saucepan with butter, sugar and salt. Cook on medium heat, stirring constantly, until mixture begins to boil. Remove and cool. Add wine and nutmeg, mixing thoroughly with beater. Spoon or pour this mixture into pie shell and top with whipped cream.

FIGS

Figs belong to a family of plants containing more than 2,000 species. They are most abundant in the tropics and subtropics, but included in the family are several kinds of mulberries that grow in temperate regions. Both breadfruits and jackfruit, important vegetables in warm climates, belong to this family. Hemp, a fiber plant that is also a source of the narcotic marijuana, and hops, used in flavoring beer, come from plants of this family. A characteristic of these plants is their production of a milky latex. South American rubber trees of this family were the first source of commercial rubber. Throughout southern Florida and the subtropics many kinds of so-called "rubber" trees are grown primarily as ornamentals.

Figs are not grown in large commercial quantities in Florida or in nearby regions. Fresh figs are available occasionally in local markets, however, and many people incorporate one or several fig trees in their landscaping. Fresh figs are a genuine taste delight and are distinctly different from the canned or dried varieties. They can be eaten out of hand, or they can be peeled and eaten with sugar and milk. They can be added to other fruits in desserts or salads, or they make an excellent topping for ice cream. If a tree produces more than can be eaten fresh, part of the crop can be preserved for later use. A very simple method is suggested here.

Fig Preserves

Wash figs thoroughly and weigh. Use a pound of sugar and a cup of water for each pound of figs, placing these ingredients in a large kettle. Cook until temperature is about 220 degrees. Cover and allow to stand overnight. Pack in sterilized jars, pouring over the figs the heated syrup from the kettle to fill the jars. For only a few jars and if the figs are to be eaten fairly soon, these can simply be placed in the refrigerator. To store for longer periods, place the filled jars in a kettle with caps in place but not screwed down tightly. Simmer for about 15 minutes, then fasten tops tightly. A dash of cinnamon, mace, and several slices of lime can be added to each jar before pouring in the syrup to give the preserves an added spicy flavor.

ANNONAS

All of the fruits described below are members of the custard-apple family, most abundantly represented in the tropics and subtropics. The only fruit-producing member of the family in temperate regions of North America is the pawpaw, which grows wild and is much esteemed for its banana-like flavor. The pawpaw has been grown successfully for commercial production on a limited scale but has never been well enough received in markets to make the effort worthwhile. In Brazil and other warm countries, there are similar fruits of this family that are popular locally but not well enough known to be produced commercially. Those listed here are the most common. They are much better known and more popular in the subtropics than in Florida, where they are available from "yard" plantings in the extreme southern part of the state.

Cherimoyas are eaten raw, either alone or in combination with other fruits. They are also used to make drinks or sherbets. Not uncommonly, the cherimoya is referred to as the "ice cream" fruit.

Cherimoyas grow best in the cool, mountainous regions of Central and South America, but there are a few plantings in Florida where those who know this fruit persist in trying, despite their production of smaller, less flavorful fruit than in good growing areas. A good cherimoya is so tasty that they feel their efforts are worth it. The flesh is custard-like in consistency and has a flavor like a banana and pineapple combined. In the most common of the several varieties, the flesh is creamy white, but there are also varieties with pink flesh. In regions where the fruit does best, the fruit may weigh four or five pounds each, occasionally as much as 10 or 12 pounds.

Soursops, or guanabanas, grow in the same geographical area as the cherimoya but at lower altitudes. They are produced successfully in extreme southern Florida but mainly as "yard" trees. Soursops are large, weighing as much as four pounds. The creamy white, often cottony, flesh has numerous brownish seeds scattered throughout. The flavor is good, but not as delicate as that of the cherimoya or the sweetsop. The fruit can be eaten raw, sweetened with sugar or honey, or it can be served with other fruits. It can also be stewed, with sugar added for sweetening. Its most popular use, however, is as a flavoring for ice cream or sherbets. In the subtropics, the fruit is pulverized and strained (to eliminate the fibers), then mixed with rum, brandy, or milk to make a beverage. Soursops can also be cooked to make jellies and jams.

Sweetsops, or sugar apples, can be grown in southern Florida. They are cultivated in many regions of the American subtropics, where they are native, and have also been introduced to other regions of the world. The fruit is much smaller than the soursop, and the outer surface is covered with a bluish "bloom" that is easily rubbed off. The creamy, custard-like flesh is delightfully aromatic and very sweet, requiring no sugar. Most of the fruit are eaten raw, but they can also be used to flavor ice cream and beverages.

Custard apples, also called bullock's hearts or jamaica apples, are grown in southern Florida, the Bahamas, and the islands of the

Caribbean. The fruit is similar in texture to the sweetsop but is not quite as good in flavor. The custard apple has been hybridized with the cherimoya to produce a plant called the atemoya, hopefully to obtain larger, more flavorful fruit that will grow in regions where the cherimoyas will not.

AVOCADOS

These natives of the American tropics and subtropics are now grown in warm regions around the world. Because of their bland flavor, the rich, buttery fruits are used both as vegetables and as desserts. Their use as vegetables is described elsewhere in the book.

Avocado-Ice Cream Whip

    1 medium to large avocado
    1 lime, juice of
    2 ½ tsp. sugar
    1 pt. vanilla ice cream

Peel avocado and remove seed. Place in electric blender, adding lime juice, sugar and ice cream. Blend until smooth. Put in tray and place in freezer. Eat just before frozen solid.

Avocado Ice Cream

    1 large or 2 medium avocados
    2 eggs
    ½ lb. sugar
    1 pt. milk
    ½ tsp. vanilla flavoring

Add milk and half the sugar to the eggs, which have been beaten lightly. Cook in a double boiler, stirring constantly until the mixture thickens. Add vanilla, stirring it throughout, and allow to cool. Using beater or low speed on electric blender, mix the avocado with this custard, adding the remaining sugar. Place in tray in freezer. When mixture has become mushy, remove and beat once again. Return to tray and freezer.

For a variation, use half honey and half sugar. Also, almond extract can be substituted for the vanilla.

Avocado Fruit Salad

1 medium-sized avocado
1 orange
1 pineapple
1 mango
1 grapefruit
1 banana
1 cantaloupe

Cut avocado in half, remove seed and peel. Cut into wedges and mix with the sectioned grapefruit and orange, diced pineapple and mango, sliced banana, and cantaloupe balls. Watermelon or honeydew melon can be used, as can cherries or grapes. The important point is that the avocado can be blended with almost any fresh fruits. A very simple combination is avocado, pineapple, and grapefruit.

Toppings can also be varied—from honey to sour cream. Some people prefer French dressing. The salad can also be sprinkled liberally with freshly grated coconut.

LOQUATS

A native of China, this small, handsome tree is now grown in many warm regions of the world. Florida is ideal. In southern Florida, the trees flower and bear fruit the year around. The trees can be pruned to shape them as desired. The leaves are shiny green above and covered with whitish down on the undersurface. The numerous fragrant white flower produce yellowish-orange, pear-shaped fruits about three inches long. They can be eaten fresh, stewed, or made into preserves or jelly. Loquats are not found regularly in markets, but the trees are commonly grown as ornamentals and for their fruit. Finding a supply should be no problem.

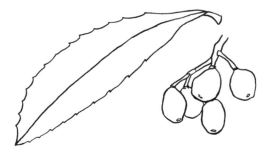

Loquat Preserves

> 1 lb. loquats
> ¾ lb. sugar
> ¾ pint water

Prepare fruit by washing, peeling, and removing seeds. Make a syrup of the sugar and water, then add fruit and cook until the temperature is about 225 degrees F. Pour into hot, sterilized jars. Place lids on loosely and simmer in the jars for about 15 additional minutes before sealing.

To make jam, use only ½ pint of water. Also, put the fruit through a chopper or blender before cooking.

STRAWBERRIES

Compared to many fruits, strawberries have been cultivated only in recent times, though wild strawberries were harvested long before recorded history. Numerous commercial varieties have been developed for the production of berries at different seasons and in soils that range from sands to black loams. South Florida grows quantities of strawberries for the winter market, and as the weather warms, the growing areas progress northward. Both visitors and residents can take advantage of the production peaks in their areas.

The uses of strawberries in Florida do not differ from the ways they are eaten in other regions, except for their companionships with subtropical fruits. Most are sugared and eaten fresh. They can be topped with whipped cream or used as a topping themselves for ice cream. While they are abundant, they can be frozen or made into preserves.

Strawberry-Pineapple Preserves

1 qt. strawberries
2 cups diced pineapple
sugar
1 orange

Wash and stem berries. Drain juice from pineapple. Slice orange very thinly. Combine the fruit and weigh. Add an equal weight of sugar, and then cook very slowly until the mixture thickens. Pour into heated jars or glasses and seal tops with melted paraffin.

Strawberry Pie

1 qt. strawberries
1 cup sugar
2 tbsp. cornstarch
whipped cream
2 tsp. lime juice
¼ tsp. salt
½ cup water
1 9-inch pie shell

Wash and stem berries. Place all except 1 cup in refrigerator to chill. Mash the strawberries, adding salt, sugar, and ¼ cup of water. Heat to boiling, adding the remaining water and the cornstarch. Stir and continue to cook until the mixture becomes clear. Remove from heat, strain, and place in refrigerator to cool. When the whole berries (or they can be cut in half) and the cooked mixture are cool, add lime juice to cooked mixture and pour over chilled berries. Spoon into pie shell and top with whipped cream.

CALABAZAS

Calabazas can be used like pumpkins or other members of the squash family to make desserts, or they can be cooked as vegetables (see page 190).

Calabaza Pudding

    2 cups of calabaza, cooked and mashed
    4 eggs
    2 tsp. cinnamon
    2 tbsp. butter
    1 tsp. nutmeg
    ⅓ cup of flour
    ⅓ cup of sugar
    2 cups of milk

Put mashed calabaza in a greased glass casserole dish. Add eggs, cinnamon, butter, nutmeg, flour, sugar, and milk. Mix thoroughly. Put dish in oven preheated to 400 degrees. Excellent with ice cream. Serves 3-4.

Calabaza Pie

    1 ½ cups cooked, mashed calabaza
    ¾ cup sugar
    ½ tsp. salt
    2 tsp. cinnamon

½ tsp nutmeg
1 tsp. ginger
½ tsp. cloves
3 eggs, lightly beaten
1 ¼ cups milk
1 6-oz. can evaporated milk
1 unbaked 10-inch pie shell

Combine all but last four ingredients. Then blend in eggs, milk, and evaporated milk. Pour into pie shell and bake for 50 minutes in oven preheated to 400 degrees. Test with knife. If knife comes out clean when inserted about halfway between center and edge, pie is done. If not, allow another 5 minutes, then test again. Cool before serving.

COCOPLUMS

Cocoplums grow wild in southern Florida and throughout most of the Caribbean area. They are not produced commercially, for the small, white-fleshed fruit are not especially appealing except in jellies and preserves. In the Bahamas and islands in the south, they are regularly utilized in this manner, less so in Florida. The fruit is peeled, then cooked with an equal weight of sugar. If the result is too sweet, lime juice can be added. If the large seed is punctured with a knife, letting the sweet syrup inside, the seeds can then be eaten with the fruit pulp. In some areas, the seeds are removed, roasted, and eaten like nuts.

TAMARINDS

This native of tropical Africa and southeastern Asia is a member of the legume or pea family. The tree becomes large and is often grown as an ornamental and shade tree as well as for the fruit. In the tropics, the fine-grained wood of the tree is used for furniture and cabinets. Tamarind trees grow well in southern Florida as well as in regions to the south. In their favor, the trees are more stable in hurricanes than are many others.

The tamarind fruit is a stubby, beanlike pod, two to six inches long. Constrictions along the pod show the locations of the seeds. Young, green, immature pods are highly acid. They are cooked in rice or are used to season meats or fish. When mature but not yet brown and dried, they are shelled, and the dark, pasty pulp is eaten. It is tart and datelike. Mature fruits can be shelled and the pulp cooked in sugar water, which is then strained to eliminate the solids. The liquid can be diluted with water as desired to make a refreshing drink—tamarind-ade. The pulp is also added to chutney or other meat sauces. A flavorful vinegar can be made by adding several shelled tamarinds and one or two cloves of garlic to the vinegar bottle.

CARAMBOLAS

The carambola, from southeastern Asia originally, is now grown in southern Florida and the Caribbean. The trees are handsome ornamentals, and the fruits are unusual in appearance—translucent yellow with a shiny, waxlike skin and four or five prominent ribs. When cut in cross section, the fruits are distinctly star-shaped. The fruit has an appealing odor and, depending on the variety, is sweet to acid in flavor. The attractive slices are excellent on breakfast cereals, and the juice makes a refreshing drink. Carambolas can also be cooked to make preserves, jams and jellies that have a tart, quincelike flavor. Because of their popularity, carambolas now appear in markets regularly from commercial plantings.

Carambola Pie

1 qt. of carambola, cut into bite-sized pieces.
¾ cup honey
¼ cup minute tapioca
2 tbsp. butter
2 tsp. nutmeg
2 tsp. cinnamon
butter
2 9-inch pie crusts and pastry for tops

Prepare ripe carambolas by cutting off edges of ridges and removing seeds while cutting into pieces. Combine honey and tapioca and mix in the carambola pieces. Spread fruit, honey, and tapioca mixture over pie shells in pans, sprinkling both with nutmeg and cinnamon. Place small pieces of butter over fruit. Put pastry over top, sealing at edges. With a fork, cut gashes in pastry to allow steam to escape. Bake for 30 to 35 minutes, or until golden brown, in an oven preheated to 425 degrees. Serve either hot or cold.

CUCUMBER TREE, OR BILIMBI

Closely related to the carambola, the cucumber tree is from tropical Asia. There are only a few of these trees in southern Florida. They are extremely sensitive to cold when young, and so they do best in the warmer Caribbean. The dark red flowers and the fruit are borne in clusters on the trunk of the tree and at the bases of larger branches. The fruit are thin-skinned and greenish, looking much like small cucumbers; they are slightly five-angled, like the carambola. The most common variety is made into jelly or preserved in a sugar syrup. The juice of the ripe fruit makes a refreshing drink. Mature but still firm and highly acid fruits make an excellent companion to meat or fish. Eaten like pickles.

CITRUS FRUITS

Several dozen species and varieties of citrus fruits grow in warm regions. In Florida, the main citrus growing area is in the central part of the state, but throughout the state and in the Caribbean, there are numerous smaller plantings of citrus for commercial production. Many people have one to several trees in their yard to supply household needs. Listed here are the principal kinds of citrus and a few of the varieties.

Sweet Oranges probably came originally from China. They are no longer known in the wild. Among the dozen or more varieties in Florida, the most prominent are the Hamlin, Pineapple, Valencia, Navel, and Temple.

Sour Oranges, also from southeastern Asia, have thick skins and a sour pulp that is used mainly in making marmalade. The trees are hardy and are often used as rootstock for sweet orange varieties.

Tangerines, or mandarins, originally from southeastern Asia, are a kind of citrus that are easily peeled and the pulp separated into sections. There are a number of varieties of different sizes and flavors. Temple oranges, for example, peel easily and are probably a hybrid of a sweet orange with a mandarin. King oranges are probably also hybrids. One of the recently developed and popular varieties is the Murcott. Tangelos are hybrids of tangerines and grapefruit.

Limes, from the East Indies but now grown in warm regions around the world, are usually picked when their skins are still green, but they do turn yellow when fully mature. The most common commercial variety is the Persian or Tahitian, which is green fleshed and about the size of a lemon. The Key or Mexican lime is much smaller. It is grown only in the Keys or on the islands fringing the southern part of the state. There are a few scattered plantings on the mainland—but no commercial groves. These little limes are also grown on the islands of the Caribbean. They are highly aromatic and are also filled with juice.

Lemons, from southeastern Asia, grow best where the summers are dry, hence are not produced commercially in Florida. Many people do have productive dooryard plantings, however. There are a number of varieties of lemons, with differences in quality as well as size. Some kinds of lemons are grown principally as ornamentals or as oddities because of the large size and rough textured skins of the fruit.

Pummelos, or shaddocks, from southeastern Asia, look like volleyball sized grapefruit, of which they may be an ancestor. The pulp is much inferior to the grapefruit, though some sweet-fleshed varieties have been developed. The thick peels of the pummelo are candied.

Grapefruit are believed to be natives of the West Indies, probably originating in Jamaica as a mutant of the Pummelo. A number of varieties have been developed, including both seedless and pink-fleshed kinds.

Citrons, natives of India and southeastern China, are not grown commercially in Florida, but there are many dooryard plantings. Citrons look like oversized lemons. They have thick skin, which may be candied, and only a small amount of pulp.

The various citrus fruits have literally countless uses in salads, desserts, and drinks. Here are a few suggestions to stimulate more exploration.

Kumquats are close relatives of the citrus fruits. The bright orange, oval fruits are attractive as ornamentals as well as being edible. In most varieties, the pulp is sour, but the skins are sweet. Limequats, hybrids of kumquats and limes, are grown in limited quantities.

Calamondins, also relatives of the citrus, are grown as ornamentals, like kumquats. The fruit is sour and is sometimes substituted for limes or lemons. They make an excellent marmalade. Alone or combined with lime juice, orange juice, or other juice, they contribute to a delightfully refreshing drink.

Orange Ice Cream

    4 cups fresh orange juice
    1 ¼ cups sugar
    1 cup thick cream
    3 cups milk

Mix orange juice and sugar, then add the cream and milk. Pour into tray and freeze.

Orange Sherbet

    1 6-oz. can frozen orange juice, undiluted
    ¾ cup sugar
    1 tbsp. lime juice
    1 tsp. almond flavoring
    ½ cup dry milk
    2 egg whites, beaten stiff but not dry

Blend sugar in ¾ cup water in saucepan over medium heat. Bring to a boil, then reduce heat and simmer for 10 minutes. Put almond flavoring and lime juice in ½ cup of water in mixing bowl. Sprinkle dry milk over top and then beat with mixer until thick and fluffy. This may take 8-10 minutes. Blend in the undiluted frozen orange juice. Add the previously made syrup, stirring constantly. You will have enough to fill 2 ice cube trays. Place in freezer. When partially frozen, remove and break up with a fork. Beat with mixer, then fold in the stiffly beaten egg whites. Return to freezer and allow to freeze firmly. Serves 10-12.

Baked Oranges

1 orange per serving
butter
powdered sugar
brown sugar
heavy cream

Wash oranges and place in saucepan or kettle. Cover with water and cook on medium heat until skins are tender. Drain, slice off tops of oranges and save. Remove cores from each orange. Place oranges in casserole dish, putting 1 tsp. butter and 1 tbsp. of brown sugar in the center of each. Replace top and sprinkle with powdered sugar. Pour small amount of water into casserole dish, just enough to cover the bottom. Put casserole in oven at 350 degrees for about 30 minutes. Pour cream over the top before serving. For a variation, remove cores from orange as above, then scoop out the pulp and mix with dates, shredded coconut, and chopped pecans or walnuts. Refill oranges and bake as above. Remove tops and stuff in one or two marshmallows, then return to oven for 5 minutes.

Orange Nut Rolls

2 tsp. grated orange rind
4 tbsp. orange juice
3 eggs
½ lb. cake flour
½ cup chopped pecans
¼ lb. sugar

¼ lb. butter
1 tbsp. baking powder
1 tsp. salt

Mix butter and sugar, adding eggs one at a time until mixture is creamy. Add the sifted flour, salt, and baking powder, pouring in the orange juice a bit at a time and stirring thoroughly. Finally, add the grated orange rind and the chopped nuts, stirring thoroughly. Place on greased baking sheet a spoonful at a time and bake at 350 degrees. This makes about 24 small rolls.

Orange Soufflé

1 cup orange juice
½ cup sugar
½ cup flour, sifted
1 tbsp. lime juice
1 tbsp. grated orange rind
4 eggs

Add orange juice to flour slowly, mixing until smooth. Cook on medium heat until mixture thickens. Add egg yolks and beat, then add lime juice, grated orange rind, and half of the sugar, mixing thoroughly. Mix the remaining sugar with the egg whites and beat until stiff. Fold the mixture together in a buttered casserole and bake for 30 minutes at 400 degrees.

The above should be served with a light citrus sauce made by simmering 1 ½ tsp. grated orange rind in 1 cup of water for about 10 minutes, then adding 1 cup of orange juice and 1 tbsp. of cornstarch that have been mixed with a small amount of cold water to make a paste. Stir these ingredients thoroughly and simmer for about 5 minutes.

Orange Cream Pie

2 tbsp. grated orange rind
2 tbsp. lime juice
1 ½ cups orange juice

2 eggs, yolks and white separated
⅔ cup sugar
1 package unflavored gelatin
¼ tsp. salt
¼ tsp. cream of tartar
1 cup whipped cream
9-inch pie shell

Combine gelatin with salt and half the sugar. Beat egg yolks with orange juice and add to the gelatin. Cook over low heat, stirring constantly, until all of the gelatin has dissolved and the mixture is slightly thickened. Remove from heat and stir in the grated orange rind and the lime juice. Chill, stirring several times. Add cream of tartar to egg whites and beat until frothy, adding sugar a bit at a time. When mixture is stiff, fold into the gelatin mixture. Also fold in the whipped cream. When all are thoroughly blended, pour into pie shell and chill.

Orange Ice

2 cups orange juice
¼ cup lime juice
grated orange rind from 2 oranges
2 cups sugar
4 cups water

Add sugar to water and heat to boiling. Allow to cool, then stir in the orange juice and the grated orange rind. Blend in electric blender or beat vigorously. Pour into tray and place in freezer. When this becomes mushy, remove and beat it again; then replace in tray and freeze. This can be served in dessert or sherbet dishes, or for a more unique presentation, serve in hollowed-out, cooled orange halves.

Orange Milk

1 qt. milk
1 pt. fresh orange juice

Pour cold milk into glass to about ⅔ full, then add cold orange juice to fill. Stir. This is different, simple, and surprisingly good.

Orange Juice Cocktail

4 oranges
1 tsp. lime juice
½ cup strawberries
½ cup finely diced or crushed fresh pineapple
sugar

Cut tops from oranges. Remove cores and spoon out the pulp. Mix orange pulp with the strawberries and the pineapple, adding sugar to taste (or use honey rather than sugar). Fill scooped-out orange hulls with this mixture and chill. Set in crushed ice in sherbet dishes for serving. Serves 4.

Hot Orange Juice Punch

2 6-oz. cans frozen orange juice
6 cans water
3 cups orange-pineapple juice
1 ½ cups sugar
½ tsp. cloves
2 sticks cinnamon
6 thin slices of orange, for garnish

Combine all ingredients, except orange slices and cloves, in a saucepan and bring to a boil. Simmer for 4-5 minute, then strain. Pour into a punch bowl or pitcher. Stud the orange slices with cloves and float them on top. Provides 18-20 glasses of drink, which should be served warm.

Orange Candy

1 6-oz. can frozen orange juice, undiluted
1 ½ cups sugar
1 cup shelled walnuts or pecans

½ *cup dates*
¼ *cup maraschino cherries*

Put undiluted orange juice in saucepan. Blend in sugar while stirring over medium heat until a soft ball forms when a spoon of the mixture is dropped into cold water. Remove from heat and stir, adding nuts and cherries. Pour mixture onto a greased cookie sheet, and when cool, form into balls for eating or for stuffing into dates or prunes.

Orange Sponge

1 cup orange juice
1 tbsp. plain gelatin
¼ cup cold water
⅓ cup sugar
⅛ tsp. salt
2 tsp. lime juice
½ tsp. orange rind, grated
2 egg whites

Soften gelatin in cold water for about 5 minutes, then add sugar, salt, and orange juice plus 1 cup of boiling water. Stir to make sure all are dissolved. As soon as partly congealed, beat with mixer until fluffy. Fold in egg whites, which have already been stiffly beaten. Chill until firm (5-6 hours), then enjoy! Serves 4-5.

Orange Juice Glazed Rolls

1 cup orange juice
2 tbsp. grated orange peel
2 tbsp. butter or margarine
1 cup sugar
1 tbsp. melted butter or margarine
½ tsp. cinnamon
1 package roll mix
½ cup pecan halves (optional)

Prepare roll mix as directed on package—but add 1 tbsp. grated orange peel. In saucepan, mix remaining orange peel with ⅔ cup sugar, orange juice, and 1 tbsp. melted butter (or margarine). Boil for 4–5 minutes. Add pecans, if used. Pour this thickened syrup into compartments of muffin pan, dividing equally. This is enough for 1 ½ dozen rolls. Form roll mix into a stick about 18 inches long. Spread with butter and sprinkle with cinnamon and the remaining sugar. Roll, fold, and then cut into pieces about an inch thick. Put each into cooled orange syrup in muffin pan compartments and allow to rise for about 1 hour—or until roughly twice original size. Bake for 20–25 minutes in oven preheated to 375 degrees.

Orange Puffs

2 cups orange juice
½ lb. flour
½ tsp. salt
2 tbsp. butter
2 tbsp. sugar
powdered sugar, if desired

Mix all ingredients (except powdered sugar) to make a smooth dough, adding cold water as necessary. Roll dough to as thin as possible, then cut into strips, squares, circles, or whatever shapes preferred. Fry in deep fat until brown. Drain and eat. Can be sprinkled with powdered sugar before serving.

Orange Oatmeal Cookies

½ cup orange juice
2 cups flour
1 tsp. baking soda
¾ tsp. salt
½ tsp. ground cinnamon
⅛ tsp. allspice
1 cup shortening
½ cup sugar

½ *cup light brown sugar*

2 *eggs*

2 *cups quick-cooked rolled oats*

1 *cup seedless raisins*

2 *tsp. grated orange peel*

½ *cup nuts (walnuts or pecans)*

Sift flour with soda, salt, and spices—at least three times. Beat shortening until smooth and soft. Add sugar and also brown sugar, beating until very light. Stir in the oats. Add flour mixture and the orange juice in two or three portions, beating well after each addition. Stir in raisins, nuts, and grated orange peel. Place by tablespoonful on greased baking sheet and bake 10-12 minutes in oven preheated to 350 degrees. This should make about 8 dozen cookies.

Key Lime Pie

juice of 3 limes or about ½ cup (Key limes preferred, but Persian can be used)

1 *cup (1 14-oz. can) sweetened condensed milk*

4 *egg yolks*

whipped cream

1 *9-inch pie shell*

Mix the condensed milk, egg yolks, and the lime juice, stirring until thickened and blended. Pour into pie shell and chill in refrigerator for about 3 hours. Top with whipped cream. Or meringue can be used in place of whipped cream.

Lime Juice Cocktail

4 *tbsp. lime juice*

2 *tbsp. orange juice*

sugar

⅔ *cup ginger ale*

crushed ice

Place juices, ginger ale, and sugar in cocktail shaker and shake thoroughly. Pour over crushed ice.

For a variation, add grapefruit juice.

Limeade with Grape Juice

> juice of 5 limes
> 2 cups grape juice
> 3 cups of cold water
> 1 cup sugar

Place water in pitcher and add sugar, stirring thoroughly. Add grape juice and then the lime juice, again stirring. Add ice to cool. Use more sugar if necessary, or if too sweet, add a bit more lime juice.

Limeade

> juice of 6 limes
> ⅓ cup sugar
> crushed ice
> cold water

Combine sugar with 1 cup of water in saucepan. Heat and stir until sugar is dissolved. Cool. Add lime juice. Fill six tall glasses with crushed ice and pour equal portions of lime juice-sugar water mixture into each glass. Add water to fill. Carbonated water can be used if desired. For a garnish, add a sprig of mint and a slice of lime.

Lime-Papaya Marmalade

> 2 cups fresh lime juice
> 1 tbsp. pineapple juice
> 3 lbs. of papaya pulp
> 1 qt. strained honey

Place the papaya pulp, lime juice, pineapple juice, and honey in blender and mix thoroughly. Pour into a saucepan and cook on low heat until the mixture thickens. Place in jars and seal tightly.

For this small a quantity, the jars can be stored in the refrigerator.

Lime Sherbet

> *juice of 6 limes*
> *⅔ cup sugar*
> *1 tsp. gelatin*
> *2 egg whites*
> *⅛ tsp. salt*
> *1 ½ cups water*

Combine the sugar and water, stirring as the water is brought to a boiling point and the sugar dissolves. Simmer for 10 minutes. Add gelatin (softened with a small amount of water), stirring until it dissolves completely. Chill. Add the lime juice and pour into a tray. Place in freezer. When mixture is half frozen, fold in the salt and egg whites that have been beaten until stiff. Replace in the tray and put in freezer. When this becomes mushy, remove and stir again. Return to freezer. Serve when completely frozen.

Note: Lemon sherbet can be prepared in the same manner using lemon juice instead of lime juice.

Lemon Pie

> *⅓ cup lemon juice*
> *1 lemon rind, grated*
> *3 eggs*
> *1 9-inch pie shell*
> *3 tbsp. hot water*
> *¼ tsp. salt*
> *1 cup sugar*

Beat egg yolks lightly, then add the lemon juice, grated rind, hot water, salt and ½ cup sugar. Cook this mixture in a double boiler until it thickens. Add the remaining ½ cup of sugar to stiffly beaten egg whites. Fold into the cooked mixture and then spoon into the pie shell. Place in oven at moderate heat for about 10 minutes. Top with meringue or with whipped cream if desired.

Lemon Eggnog

½ cup lemon juice
1 ½ cups milk
2 cups cold water
3 eggs
½ cup sugar
grated nutmeg

Combine the eggs, sugar, milk, and water, mixing thoroughly with a beater. Add lemon juice and stir again. Serve in glasses, topping with nutmeg. The above will make about 4 glasses of eggnog.

Grapefruit-Grape Salad

2 grapefruit, pulp removed and diced
1 bunch grapes, washed and cut in half lengthwise
1 ½ tbsp. creamy salad dressing
½ cup pecans, shelled and coarsely chopped
½ cup small marshmallows, or large ones diced

Mix the fruits, nuts, and marshmallows. Coat them thoroughly with the salad dressing. Add more dressing if necessary. Place individual servings on lettuce leaf. Serves 3-4.

Broiled Grapefruit

½ grapefruit for each serving
honey
cinnamon
butter
sugar

Cut grapefruit in half and run knife between sections and around peel to free the sections for easy eating. Remove core and some of the surrounding pulp to make a hole in the center. Fill hole with honey and 1 tsp. of butter. Sprinkle top with sugar and cinnamon. Place under broiler until top begins to brown. This will require only a few minutes. Or grapefruit can be baked (rather than broiled) for 15-20 minutes in oven preheated to 400 degrees.

Grapefruit with Rum

½ grapefruit per serving
sugar
white rum

Remove pulp from grapefruit halves. Save the cleaned-out shells. Place pulp in bowl and add 4 tbsp. of rum for each half of grapefruit. Sugar the mixture to taste and allow to marinate for about 2 hours at room temperature. Before serving, heat the pulp and rum mixture and replace in the hollowed-out shells.

Grapefruit and Fruit Baskets

2 grapefruit (to serve 4 people)
1 orange
1 small avocado
1 mango, carambola, or other fruit
creamy salad dressing
maraschino cherries

Cut the grapefruit in half and remove sections carefully. Dice. Clean out the grapefruit shells and cut points or scallops into the edges of each to make attractive serving bowls. Combine all of the fruits, coating them with salad dressing. Place in the carved skins, topping each with a maraschino cherry.

Candied Grapefruit Peels

Cut grapefruit peels into strips about a quarter of an inch wide. Place in a saucepan and cover with cold water. Bring to a boil, then drain. Repeat this 5 times, using fresh water each time. This will eliminate bitterness in the peel. Weigh the peels and then add an equal weight of sugar to peels and just enough water to cover them. Cook on low heat and toss until the sugar is completely dissolved. Simmer until this sugar syrup begins to form into soft balls. Remove the peels and roll each in granulated sugar on wax paper. Cool and dry thoroughly, then store in jars in refrigerator.

Grapefruit Supreme

2 grapefruit (for 4 servings)
12 marshmallows
3 tsp. lime juice
1 egg white (2 if eggs are small)
salt
vanilla ice cream

Cut grapefruit in half, removing pulp. Clean the shells. Sprinkle the pulp with sugar to taste, replace in shells, and put in the refrigerator to cool. In double boiler, melt the marshmallows in the lime juice, stirring until smooth. Cool. Beat the egg whites, adding a pinch of salt, until mounded peaks form. Add about 1 tsp. of sugar and continue to beat until stiff. Complete the filling of the shells with ice cream and then cover with meringue. Place under broiler for 1-2 minutes to brown tops. Serve immediately.

Grapefruit-Cider Punch

3 cups grapefruit juice
3 cups sweet cider
½ cup sugar
½ cup lime juice
2 cups water

Combine all ingredients, stirring thoroughly. Chill before serving. Garnish with slices of apple or lime if desired.

Grapefruit-Honey Drink

Mix three parts grapefruit juice with one part honey. Stir thoroughly and chill before serving.

Grapefruit-Orange-Lime Marmalade

1 grapefruit, pulp
1 lime, pulp
2 oranges, pulp and grated peel

Put grated orange peel and pulp of all fruits in food chopper. Add three times as much water to chopped pulp and boil for about 15 minutes. Allow to stand overnight. Boil for additional 10 minutes, then cool. Add sugar in amount equal to weight of cooked fruit. Cook at 220 degrees until reaches jelly stage. Pour into jars and seal. Or store in refrigerator for immediate use.

Calamondin Marmalade

2 qts. calamondins
2 tbsp. baking soda
sugar
pectin (optional)

Wash fruit and place in large kettle, adding the baking soda and boiling water to cover. Place lid on kettle and allow to stand for about 15 minutes. Pour off water and rinse fruit several times. Cut calamondins and remove seeds. Put fruit through coarse grinder (or chop coarsely with knife). Place fruit in pressure cooker, adding 3 cups of water for each cup of fruit. Cook for 3 minutes at 10 pounds pressure. Cool. For each three cups of cooked calamondins, add 3 cups of sugar and 1 tsp. of pectin (optional). Add sugar (pectin mixed with it if used) slowly. Boil mixture for about 20 minutes, or until reaches jelly stage. Remove from heat and cool. Pour into sterilized jars and seal.

Calamondin Pie

½ cup calamondin juice
1 can condensed, sweetened milk
3-4 egg yolks

Combine and put in 9-inch graham cracker pie crust. Whip egg whites until stiff, adding 2 tbsp. of sugar while whipping. Spread on top as a meringue. Put in oven preheated to 350 degrees and cook until meringue turns golden brown. This will take about 15 minutes. Serve well chilled.

Can use pie filling as a custard without baking if desired.

Kumquat Preserves

1 ¼ lbs kumquats
1 lb. sugar

Wash kumquats thoroughly, then sprinkle with 1 tbsp. soda for each quart of kumquats. Pour boiling water over the fruit and allow to stand for about 15 minutes. Rinse through three or four waters. Slit each fruit to the seed, place in kettle, cover with water, and bring to a boil, cooking until fruit is tender. Drain. Add sugar in 3 ½ cups of water. Bring to a boil, stirring to make certain the sugar is completely dissolved. Drop the kumquats into this boiling sugar solution and bring to boil again, making certain the temperature reaches 220 degrees. Remove from heat, cover kettle, and allow to stand for about 20 minutes. Repeat and then pack the fruit into jars, pouring the syrup around them to fill jars completely. Seal jars tightly.

BARBADOS CHERRIES

This small West Indian cherry came into prominence a few years ago when it was discovered to be probably the richest source of natural vitamin C, or ascorbic acid. One small cherry may contain as much as 40 times more vitamin C than the average orange. The fruits are too sour for most people to eat raw, but the juice can be added to other fruit juices for vitamin enrichment. The fruit are also used to make preserves or jellies. There are only a few commercial plantings of the Barbados cherry, and the crop is processed mainly for juices rather than being sold in the markets. Dooryard plantings are fairly common in southern

Florida, however, for the bushy trees, about 15 feet tall, make excellent screens while also bearing crops of fruit in spring and fall.

BIGNAYS

Bignays are not as common in Florida as they are in the islands of the Caribbean. They are not grown commercially but may be used as part of the landscaping. Introduced from southern Asia, the medium-sized evergreen trees produce clusters of fruit that are about half an inch in diameter. Dark reddish-purple when ripe, they are too acid for most people to eat out of hand, but they make an excellent jam or jelly.

MANGOES

Grown in southern Florida and throughout the nearby subtropics and tropics, the mango is believed to be the oldest of all the cultivated fruits. It has, in fact, been labeled the "king of the tropical fruits." Cultivation of this magnificent fruit is more ancient than recorded history. Centuries ago, Buddha was presented with an orchard of handsome mango trees so that he could rest in their shade and enjoy eating the fruit. In the early 1500s, an emperor of India ordered the planting of more than 100,000 mango trees in a single orchard to satisfy his personal craving for the delicious fruit. Even in India today, the mango figures strongly in folklore and religion. Before a mango tree's first fruit can be eaten, the tree must be ceremoniously "married" to some other tree, most often a tamarind or jasmine. The tree's owner may borrow money to the extent of bankrupting himself to make certain the marriage ceremony is carried off as elaborately as he believes his family name deserves.

Mango trees belong to the same family as the cashew nut, the pistachio, and, of all things, poison ivy. Some people are allergic to the sap, present also in the skin of the fruit. They will break out into an itchy red, pimply rash if they are near the trees in flower, walk through mango-wood smoke, or handle the fruit without washing their hands carefully.

In southern Florida, a gathering of mango growers is held every year so that new varieties can be displayed and tested. Some kinds have a pineapple-like flavor. Others resemble peaches. Still others are melon-like. The flavors are limitless, but all have the distinctive and delightful mango flavor overriding the others. The kind most resembling the original stock is stringy and has a definite turpentine flavor. It is not especially large and has a pointed or narrowed tip. Other commercial varieties weigh several pounds and are round and plump, the stringy characteristic greatly reduced. Many kinds still have green skins when mature and ready for use. Some ripen unevenly. The favorite market varieties are blushed with yellow and crimson when ripe.

The fruit can be used for cooking while it is still green, most commonly in making chutney as a condiment for meats. The flesh of the ripe or mature fruits is yellow and is rich in vitamin A. The mango's vitamin C content is highest while green. It can be eaten as dessert or used in salads. This is a fruit that can be bought in markets in season. Everyone with available space should consider having a mango tree as part of their landscaping.

All of the more than 1,000 varieties of the mango originated from a species that grew wild in the Himalayan Mountains. The mango has since been spread to warm regions around the world. It arrived in Florida just prior to the Civil War.

Most recipes here call for chopped or sliced mangoes. First peel off the skin (under a faucet if you are allergic). Cut a slice off one side so the fruit lies flat on a cutting board. Then proceed to slice fruit from all around the seed, removing as much as possible. This is a slippery job, but well worth it.

Mango Butter

6 cups of ripe or half-ripe mangoes,

48

cut fine
>   2 tbsp. lime juice
>   2 cups water
>   3 cups sugar

Cook mangoes in water until tender. If stringy, put through a sieve or fruit press. Add sugar. Cook combination until it has consistency of butter. Pour into hot, sterilized jars and seal. Immerse jars in boiling water for 10 minutes.

Mango Medley

>   1 cup diced ripe mango
>   1 cup orange sections
>   1 cup pineapple chunks, fresh or canned
>   1 cup flaked coconut
>   1 cup sour cream
>   1 cup miniature marshmallows

Combine the above and serve chilled. Note: Other fruits, such as strawberries, bananas, watermelons, papaya, or avocado, can be added if desired.

Mango Sauce

>   2 cups sliced ripe mango
>   1 tsp. lime juice
>   ½ tsp. grated lime rind
>   ¾ cup orange juice
>   6 tbsp. sugar
>   1 ½ tbsp. cornstarch
>   ¾ cup water
>   ⅛ tsp. allspice

Combine sugar, cornstarch, and salt in saucepan, then stir in orange juice and water. Add lime juice, lime rind, and allspice. Cook over medium heat. Stir until mixture thickens—in 10 to 15 minutes. Remove from heat and chill. Stir in mango slices. Serve over ice cream or cake.

Mango Chutney

  1 lb. peeled or diced green mangoes
  ½ pt. grapefruit juice
  ½ pt. vinegar
  1 lb. raisins
  ¼ lb. blanched almonds
  ¾ lb. brown sugar
  ½ cup chopped green pepper
  1 tsp. allspice
  1 clove garlic, crushed
  3 oz. sliced ginger
  1 tbsp. salt
  ½ tbsp. mustard seed
  ½ cup chopped onions
  1 tbsp. chopped hot peppers

Add sugar to vinegar and bring to a boil. Add mango and all other ingredients and bring to boil again, continuing to cook for about 30 minutes. While still boiling, pour into heated jars and seal.

  Note: This is only one version of mango chutney. Each person develops his own and seems to guard it as a family treasure. Chutney is a favorite condiment for meats throughout the tropics.

Mango Ice Cream

  1 pt. ripe mangoes, diced
  1 qt. iced milk

Blend iced milk with mangoes in electric blender and freeze.

  Note: This is the best way to preserve the mango flavor for after-season eating. If the fruit is frozen alone, it has a mushy texture when thawed and has lost much of its original flavor.

Fresh Mango Sundae

½ mango per serving
vanilla ice cream

Cut chilled mango in half and remove seed. Fill the cavity with ice cream and serve.

Mango Pie

6 green but mature mangoes
⅔ cup sugar
¼ tsp. salt
2 tbsp. flour
1 tbsp. butter
1 9-inch pie shell (not baked)

Sift the dry ingredients and mix with the sliced mangoes. Fill the pie shell with this mixture. Dot with butter and bake at 450 degrees for 15 minutes. Reduce heat to 350 degrees and continue baking for 45 minutes.

Mango Cheesecake

1 ½ cups chopped ripe mango
½ cup sugar
2 tsp. lime juice
1 pkg. plain gelatin
1 12-oz. pkg. cream cheese
¾ cup sour cream
1 tsp. vanilla
1 9-inch graham cracker pie shell

Combine mango, sugar, and lime juice in bowl. Cover and cool in refrigerator for about 30 minutes. Drain off liquid from bottom of bowl and soften gelatin in the liquid. Dissolve over hot water. Put in bowl with mango. Now beat cream cheese until light, then stir in sour cream and vanilla. Fold mango into cheese mixture. Spoon into pie shell and refrigerate until firm. Can be served with fresh slices of mango on top.

Mango Nut Bread

½ cup chopped walnuts or pecans
½ cup butter
¾ cup sugar
2 eggs
⅔ cup finely chopped ripe mango
2 cups sifted flour
1 tsp. baking soda
1 tbsp. lime juice
¼ tsp. salt
½ cup shortening or butter

Cream shortening and sugar. Add eggs, then stir in mango, lime juice, and dry ingredients. Bake in loaf pan for 1 hour in oven preheated to 375 degrees. Do not cut until completely cooled, holding until second day if possible.

Mango Tarts

4 ripe mangoes
1 tsp. cornstarch
2 egg yolks, beaten
½ cup water
1 tsp. cinnamon
1 cup sugar
2 tbsp. butter
6 tart shells, previously cooked

Slice the mangoes thinly. Heat in saucepan with water and sugar and cook at a moderate heat for 15 minutes. Mix cornstarch and egg yolks with small amount of water and add to the mango sauce. Continue to cook for several minutes, stirring constantly. Add the cinnamon and butter while stirring. Fill the previously cooked tart shells. Serve while still warm.

Mango Preserves

2 lbs. of just-ripened fruit, peeled and sliced
2 lbs. sugar
8 cups of water

Add sugar to water and bring to a boil. Add fruit and cook until clear. Allow to stand until cool, then boil—making certain the temperature exceeds 222 degrees. Let stand until cool. Pack in heated jars, simmering for about 25 minutes and then sealing.

AMBARELLAS

This close relative of the mango is widely grown in the Caribbean but is not as common in Florida. The egg-sized fruits are borne in clusters, and they vary greatly in flavor. They can be made into good jam or jelly, however, and the juice of the ripe fruit makes an excellent drink. Even the best ambarella is inferior to any mango.

LYCHEES

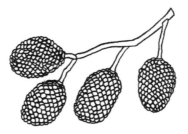

This fruit is associated with the Chinese and is thought of primarily as being eaten dried rather than fresh. It is surprising to many people to find numerous dooryard plantings of lychees in Florida and also some sizable commercial plantings along the lower west coast. Here the fruit is eaten mainly fresh. A number of varieties have been developed, not only to select those with the best flavor but also to get fruit with smaller seeds and a greater amount of flesh. In some of the earlier varieties only a thin layer of translucent flesh clings to the very large seed.

Lychee trees are medium-sized, handsome evergreens that enhance a landscape. They need copious amounts of water in well-drained, rich soil, and they grow slowly.

Most lychees are eaten out of hand, but those who have lychees in sufficient abundance to allow experimenting can try them in other ways. Peeled and seeded, lychees make an excellent addition to almost any fruit salad. To make their addition even more unique, insert a pecan into the seed cavity. The two are good companions. Lychees are sometimes substituted in martinis for the olives or onions. Good commercial varieties are much larger, hence leave less space for the beverage.

SPANISH LIMES

Spanish limes are rare on the Florida mainland, but they are grown in the Florida Keys, the Bahamas, and the Caribbean, where they are very popular. The round fruit, usually only about an inch in diameter, has a leathery green or lime-colored skin that covers the translucent flesh. They are eaten fresh, like grapes. Mamocillo and genip are other names for the Spanish lime. The tree is an attractive evergreen that is sometimes grown as an ornamental.

MANGOSTEENS

To many people, this is the best of all the fruits of the tropics and subtropics. The mangosteen is rare in Florida, but those few that are produced are consumed almost as rapidly as they ripen. Most fruits of the subtropics and tropics have an underlying flavor that is almost rancid, making them distasteful to many people. The mangosteen lacks this taste, and so it is liked immediately by almost everyone. A native of the Asiatic tropics, it is now grown in warm regions throughout the world. About three inches in diameter, it has a reddish-purple skin when ripe. The flesh is snowy white.

MAMEY

The mamey, from the American subtropics, is widely grown as a dooryard plant—to a limited extent even in southern Florida. The fragrant white flowers produce fruit that are five to eight inches in diameter. A rough-textured brown skin surrounds the yellowish to reddish-orange, apricot-flavored flesh. The mamey can be eaten raw or sliced and served with cream and sugar. It can also be baked into pies or stewed with sugar to make a sauce or preserves. When it is cooked until just tender and is still rich in color, the flavor is enhanced. Overcooked, the mamey loses it flavor. The mamey combines well with pineapples or similar fruits. A small amount of grated fresh ginger or cinnamon adds to the over-all tastiness.

CEYLON GOOSEBERRY, OR DOVYALIS

From southern Asia, the Ceylon Gooseberry is produced on a shrubby tree. The fruit, about an inch in diameter, has purplish, very acid pulp. It is used primarily when half ripe to make jelly or jam for eating with fish or meat. The closely related kei apple, from South Africa, is a larger fruit with yellowish flesh. Neither is grown in commercial quantities, but there are dooryard plantings from which the fruit can be obtained.

GOVERNOR'S PLUM

A native of tropical Africa, the governor's plum is a large shrub that bears blackish-purple plumlike fruits. They can be eaten out of hand or cooked to make jam or jelly. The thorny plants make an effective screening hedge as well as giving their bonus yield of edible fruits.

PASSION FRUITS

Passion fruits, grown in Florida and the Caribbean, are produced on woody vines that are generally planted more for their unusual waxlike flowers than for the fruit. The fruits resemble pomegranates in that each consists of a thick, hard rind surrounding numerous seeds; each seed is enveloped in an edible pulp that is best if sugared before it is eaten. The juice from the pulp is used for flavoring drinks and sherbets. The two most common kinds are the purple giant granadilla, three to four inches long and deep purple on the outside when ripe, and the yellow-fruit passion fruit, which is larger but also less flavorful.

PAPAYAS

These natives of the American tropics are now grown in warm regions around the world. They are treelike herbs that develop wood trunks as much as 30 feet tall. For easier harvesting, growers prefer those with trunks only six to eight feet tall, putting the fruit within reach. Called pawpaws in some regions of the Caribbean and fruta bombas in others, the fruit resembles melons in appearance and taste. Some are nearly as large as watermelons; others are about the size of cantaloupes. Some have rather soft flesh which is light yellow; others have a firmer, orange-yellow flesh. In some varieties, the flesh is pinkish. There is equal wide variation in the flavor of papayas. Some rank with melons or might even be better. Others have an insipid, musky flavor that makes them scarcely edible unless mixed with other fruit. In the subtropics, papayas are popular as a breakfast fruit. They are usually seasoned with lime juice and sugar or honey, though some people prefer eating them with salt and pepper. The very best varieties need no seasoning at all. Green, immature fruits are utilized as vegetables and are described as such in the vegetable section of this book.

Papayas grow quickly, bearing fruit within a year after the planting of the seed and continuing for three or four years.

whipped Papayas
1 ½ cups papaya pulp
1 lime
½ cup sugar
2 egg whites, beaten until stiff

Mix the above ingredients and cook on moderate heat for about 15 minutes. Top with whipped cream. Serves 3-4.

Papaya Sherbet

>4 cups papaya pulp
>juice of 2 limes
>2 cups sugar

Blend the above ingredients thoroughly. Taste to see if sweet enough, adding more sugar if necessary. Place in tray and freeze. Serves 4-6.

Baked Papaya

>1 papaya, mature but still firm
>juice of 1 lime
>sugar
>cinnamon

Cut papaya in half lengthwise and remove seeds. Sprinkle the exposed surface with lime juice, sugar, and cinnamon. Bake for 20 minutes. Serve while still hot. Serves 2-4.

Papaya Butter

>1 ripe papaya
>juice of 1 lime
>sugar

Peel papaya and remove seeds. Dice flesh and place in saucepan. Cover with water and cook until tender. Mash pulp, adding 1-½ cup of sugar for each cup of pulp. Also stir in 1 tbsp. of lime juice. Cook until mixture reaches 222 degrees. Pack in sterilized jars, simmering for about 15 additional minutes before sealing.

Papaya Punch

>1 ripe papaya
>1 ½ cups milk
>½ cup water
>2 cups grapefruit juice

2 tbsp. sugar

Peel papaya, remove seeds, and cut flesh into small pieces. Place in electric blender, adding milk. Blend at high speed to pulverize the papaya. Mix the water, sugar, and grapefruit juice. Add to the papaya and milk mixture. Blend at low speed. Chill before serving. Enough for 4-6 large glasses.

POMEGRANATES

The pomegranate is produced on a shrub about 20 feet tall. Most of the fruit grown in Florida is of inferior quality. They are grown mainly as oddities, for this fruit's record extends far back in history. It served people of Asia Minor's desert regions as a thirst quencher, for the pomegranate can survive and bear fruit in dry regions. The thin but tough outer rind, yellowish when ripe, surrounds numerous seeds, each encased in a transparent or pinkish sac containing a juicy pulp. Some varieties are juicier and more flavorful than others. The juice can also be used to make a refreshing beverage by mixing it with sugar and water. Grenadine, a beverage flavoring, is a thick, sweet syrup made from pomegranate juice. For a novelty too, the pomegranate is sometimes separated into its pulp sac units which are then spread through or over a fruit salad.

TROPICAL ALMONDS

Throughout the subtropics and the tropics, though not common anywhere in Florida, the tropical almond is planted as an ornamental shade tree. Each tree also produces at least two crops of nuts per year. About two inches long, the fruits have a thin layer of edible flesh surrounding the corky shells of the nuts, or kernels. These shells are hard to break because they are so spongy. Inside each is a small, flavorful kernel that can be eaten either raw or roasted.

GUAVAS

Guavas are grown throughout the American tropics and subtropics, where they are natives, and they have been introduced to other warm regions around the world. They were cultivated in the Americas long before the arrival of European explorers. There are many varieties. Some are small and seemingly all seeds; others are as large as oranges or apples and have large amounts of flesh which may be creamy white, yellow, pink, or red. The Brazilian strawberry guava, a separate species, is small, red-fleshed, and strawberry-like in taste. Some are sweet and can be eaten out of hand, like apples, or can be added to fruit salads—such as guavas, tangerine, or orange sections, and bananas mixed with a creamy dressing and served on lettuce. Others are good only when cooked. Much in their favor, guavas are rich in vitamin C—much more so than citrus.

Guava trees grow 15 to 20 feet tall. They have a smooth reddish bark, and the white flowers are fragrant.

Stuffed Guava Shells

½ guava per serving
½ orange per serving
freshly grated coconut
creamy salad dressing or mayonnaise
lettuce

Cut guavas in half, peel, and carefully scoop out seeds in the central cavity. What remains is called the guava "shell." Fill this cavity with the cut-up orange and the fresh coconut. Top with the salad dressing or mayonnaise and place on lettuce leaf for serving.

Possible variations in the stuffings are numerous. Among the favorites are pineapple and pecans; strawberries and pecans; and celery and cheese.

Baked Guavas

3 guavas (½ per person)
½ cup sugar
1 tbsp. lime juice
butter
1 tbsp. butter
2 tbsp. water
salt

Cut guavas in half and spoon out the seeds and pulp, separating seeds from the pulp. Add lime juice, sugar, and a dash of salt to the pulp, mixing thoroughly. Fill the guava halves with this mixture. Dot the top with butter and place in baking dish to which the water has been added. Cover dish and bake at 350 degrees for 25 minutes.

Guava Jelly

3 qts. guavas
sugar
lime juice

Peel and slice guavas. Place in kettle and cover with cold water. Bring to a boil and simmer for about 2 hours. Strain cooked guava pulp through sieve. When cool add 1 ½ tbsp. lime juice and 1 ½ cups of sugar to each 2 cups of guava fluid. Mix thoroughly. Cook on low heat until the mixture reaches the jelly stage. To test this, hold a spoonful of the cooking mixture over the kettle. If a single drop of the liquid forms on the underside of the spoon and falls back into the kettle, the mixture is not ready. If two drops form and do not fall back into the kettle, the jelly stage has been reached. The cooked mixture can then be poured into sterilized jars or glasses, the top sealed with paraffin.

Note: For a spicy variation, put several sticks of cinnamon, 1 tsp. of cloves and 1 tsp. of allspice in a bag and add during cooking. Remove before pouring into glasses.

SURINAM CHERRIES

From the tropics of Brazil originally, the Surinam cherry is produced on a shrubby small tree. Planted in rows, Surinams make an attractive hedge that can be pruned or shaped as desired. They grow very slowly so that the job does not have to be repeated often. The pruning does affect their fruit bearing, however.

Also called pitangas in the Caribbean, Surinam cherries are about an inch in diameter and light red to orange to almost black, depending on the variety. They are broadly and deeply ribbed and look like tiny pumpkins. Surinams can be eaten fresh, either alone or mixed with other fruits. They can also be used for pies, jam, or jelly. Because of their tartness, they make an excellent companion fruit for meats.

JABOTICABAS

Common in tropical South America, the jaboticaba is grown only sparingly in the Caribbean and in Florida, where it can be grown from the central part of the state southward. The shrubby to medium sized trees grow slowly, producing clusters of fruit that resemble grapes in flavor. Two or three crops may be produced in a season. Dark blue to blackish when ripe, the fruit can be eaten raw or made into jam or jelly.

SAPODILLAS

Found throughout the subtropics and the tropics, the sapodilla is grown also in southern Florida. The attractive, large evergreen trees were the original source of the milky latex called chicle, the main ingredient of chewing gum. The fruits are round, two or four inches in diameter, and covered with a rusty brown skin. Inside is a yellowish-brown, sugary flesh, smooth in texture in the better varieties but grainy in others. In Florida, the fruit is eaten fresh and raw, occasionally added to fruit salads. In other countries, the ripe fruits are cooked to make a sweet syrup, or they are added to breads for flavoring.

SAPOTES

Closely related to sapodillas, sapotes are produced on a tree native to the American tropics and subtropics. They are not common in Florida, mainly because the young plants are susceptible to even slight cold. Once established, however, they grow well and produce fruit for many years. Like the sapodilla, the fruit has a rusty brown skin. The somewhat grainy flesh is sweet. It can be spooned from the skin without seasoning, or some prefer to add a few drops of lime juice. Sapotes make a tasty sherbet.

STAR APPLES

Favorites in the Caribbean, star apples are also members of the same family as the sapodilla. To avoid the bitter latex in the skin, the fruit should be cut or broken in two and spooned from the shell. The sweet, white flesh is most flavorful when chilled before it is eaten. The name of the fruit comes from the starlike shape of the core which can be seen when the fruit is cut.

CANISTEL OR EGGFRUIT

Another sapodilla relative, the canistel has a mealy flesh, somewhat like a hardcooked egg. It is eaten alone or occasionally is seasoned lightly either with salt, lime juice, or butter. The sliced fruit can be served with milk and sugar, or it can be blended with iced milk and frozen to make canistel ice cream. Canistels are not produced commercially, but there are many grown as dooryard plants in the Caribbean, fewer in Florida.

CARISSA PLUMS

A tall, thorny shrub from Africa, the carissa or Natal plum is grown in southern Florida and in many areas of the Caribbean as a virtually impenetrable hedge. The fragrant white flowers produce purplish-red, plum-sized fruits that are eaten out of hand or are mixed with other fruits in salads. Cooked, they can be used in pies or to make preserves. The mature but still not ripe fruit are made into jelly.

CHAYOTES

Chayotes are most commonly eaten as vegetables, but this versatile squash is also relished as a dessert by many Latin Americans.

Baked Chayotes

3 medium-sized chayotes
1 tsp. salt
3 tsp. cornstarch
1 cup milk
1 cinnamon stick
1 lime rind
1 cup sugar
3 eggs yolks
1 tsp. vanilla
½ cup raisins
½ cup almonds
½ cup cracker meal
6 tsp. ground cinnamon

Cut chayotes in half lengthwise and boil in salted water until tender. Let them cool and then spoon out the pulp without damaging the shells. Put pulp through strainer, then into saucepan. Put milk in bowl and stir in cornstarch, cinnamon stick, sugar, and egg yolks. Mix thoroughly, then add to chayotes in saucepan. Simmer, stirring constantly until the mixture thickens. Now add vanilla and raisins. Spoon this mixture into chayote shells. Spread almonds, cracker meal, and cinnamon over the top. Bake in oven preheated to 425 degrees until golden brown. Serves 4.

MELONS

Florida produces virtually all of the various kinds of melons, turning winter into summer for visitors from the north. Cantaloupes, honeydews, watermelons, and a variety of kinds of squash—all are available to be eaten fresh or, in the case of squash, to be made into pies and similar desserts.

Cantaloupe-Mango Salad

> 2 cups diced cantaloupe
> 2 cups diced mango
> ½ cup chopped nuts
> 1 cup creamy salad dressing

Mix the above ingredients and serve chilled in sherbet dish or on a lettuce leaf. Serves 3-4.

Cantaloupe-Banana Salad

> 2 cups cantaloupe balls
> 2 cups diced bananas
> ¼ cup creamy salad dressing
> ½ cup small marshmallows, or large marshmallows quartered
> ¼ cup chopped pecans

Combine all ingredients and serve in sherbet dishes. Serves 3-4.

Cantaloupe-Watermelon Delight

> ½ cantaloupe per serving
> watermelon balls
> powdered sugar
> strawberries (or other berries)
> brandy

Remove seeds from cantaloupe halves and brush inside with brandy. Fill cavity with mixture of watermelon balls and berries. Sprinkle with powdered sugar and chill before serving.

Cantaloupe-Grapefruit Salad

½ melon per serving
½ grapefruit per serving
brown sugar
sweet sherry

Cut melon in half and remove seeds. Cut out flesh carefully, leaving rind intact. Cut grapefruit in half and remove the edible pulp, discarding the membranes. Chop the melon and grapefruit together in a bowl, mixing in the brown sugar (or honey can be substituted). Add 1 tbsp. sherry for each half of melon and allow to marinate at room temperature for about an hour. Chill and then place in the hollowed-out, chilled melon rinds for servings.

Rummed Watermelon Balls

1 watermelon
2 oranges
2 tbsp. honey
½ cup rum

Chill melon, then cut in half and remove flesh with melon-ball scoop. Place balls in bowl containing the juice of the oranges mixed with the rum and honey. Allow to marinate at room temperature for at least half an hour. Chill and serve in sherbet dishes.

PEANUTS

Peanuts can be eaten as a snack, as ingredients in main dishes (see vegetable section of this book), or in an unending variety of cookies, cakes, pies, and other deserts. The uses suggested here are simply starters. Once you become hooked on peanuts, you will become inventive.

Peanut Butter Delights

1 cup creamy peanut butter
2 cups semisweet chocolate chips
3 cups flour
2 tsp. baking soda
⅛ tsp. salt
2 cups brown sugar
1 cup shortening
1 tsp. vanilla
2 eggs

Combine flour, baking soda, and salt in bowl and set aside. In another bowl, combine brown sugar, shortening, and vanilla, then beat until creamy. Add the eggs one at a time, beating well after each egg is added. Now blend in the peanut butter. Add the flour mixture gradually, blending well. Stir in the chocolate chips. Drop this mixture by the well-rounded teaspoonful on ungreased cookie sheet. Bake for about 10 minutes in oven preheated to 375 degrees. Yields about 10 dozen cookies.

Basic Peanut Butter Cookies

1 cup smooth peanut butter
½ cup butter
½ cup sugar
½ cup brown sugar
½ tsp. vanilla
1 egg
1 ½ cups flour, sifted
¾ tsp. baking soda
½ tsp. baking powder
½ tsp. salt

Mix peanut butter with butter until creamy smooth. Add the sugars gradually and beat until mixture is light and fluffy. Add vanilla and egg and beat until thoroughly mixed. Mix the baking soda, baking powder, and salt with the flour, then mix all ingredients together thoroughly. Chill, then shape into 1-inch balls and place about 2 inches apart on cookie sheet. Flatten with fork in crisscross pattern. Bake for 10-15 minutes in oven preheated to 375 degrees. Yields about 5 dozen cookies.

Peanut Butter Pie

    ¾ cup powdered sugar
    ⅓ cup peanut butter
    ⅔ cup sugar
    3 tbsp. cornstarch
    1 tbsp. flour
    ½ tsp. salt
    3 egg yolks
    3 cups milk
    2 tbsp. butter
    1 tsp. vanilla
    9-in. baked pie shell

First cream the peanut butter and powdered sugar in a bowl and set aside. Mixture will be crumbly. Then mix all other ingredients in a saucepan, stirring constantly while cooking over medium heat until thick. Spread about ⅔ of peanut butter and sugar mixture in bottom of pie shell. Pour the custard over the top. For a meringue, beat the 3 egg whites (saved from custard) with ¼ tsp. of cream of tartar until stiff, gradually adding ¼ cup of sugar while beating. Spread meringue over the custard and then sprinkle remainder of peanut butter and sugar mixture on top. Bake until brown in oven preheated to 350 degrees.

Peanut-Banana Cake

    1 cup mashed ripe bananas
    ¾ cup chopped peanuts
    ½ cup shortening
    1 cup sugar
    2 eggs

¾ *cup milk*
2 ½ *cups all-purpose flour*
2 ½ *tsp. baking powder*
½ *tsp. salt*

Cream shortening and sugar until fluffy, then beat in the eggs. Stir in the milk and bananas. Sift flour, baking powder, and salt, then stir in the peanuts. Add the combined dry ingredients to cake batter and beat until smooth and well blended. Pour this batter into 2 greased 8-inch cake pans and bake for 30-35 minutes in oven preheated to 350 degrees. Cool in pans for 5 minutes, then loosen at edges and remove layers to cool on racks. Icing can be spread between layers and over the top before serving.

For a peanutty icing, prepare as follows:

1 *cup evaporated milk*
¼ *cup butter or margarine*
¾ *cup chopped peanuts*
3 *egg yolks*
1 *cup sugar*
½ *cup grated coconut*

Cook sugar, egg yolks, butter, and milk on low heat for 10-12 minutes, stirring constantly. Remove from heat. Add nuts and coconut and stir until thick enough to spread as icing.

HONEY

Honey is a flavorful natural sweetener and high-energy food that can be substituted for sugar for use on cereals, in drinks, and in cookery. Most of the honey bought in supermarkets is blended to make it uniform—mild in taste and light amber in color—but honey comes in as many flavors and colors as there are nectar-producing flowers. By getting acquainted with a beekeeper or finding a store that handles unblended honeys, you can experience some of these distinctive flavors. Light honeys are mild, while dark honeys have a stronger flavor but are also richer in minerals.

Among the Florida favorites are gallberry, which is water white and very mild; saw-palmetto and cabbage palm, amber and mild; tupelo, which is amber, mild, and an excellent all-purpose honey; orange blossom, medium amber and with a distinctive flavor; mangrove, very light and sweet; avocado, very dark and as heavy as cane syrup; goldenrod, a dark honey produced in autumn. And there are scores of others, all of them taste delights.

2.

Fish & Shellfish

The Florida finger of land is surrounded by waters warmed by currents from the subtropics, laced in places with colder waters from the north. The variety of seafoods available in these waters borders the fantastic, yet getting fresh seafoods in Florida is not always easy. Most of the commercial catch is processed aboard ships and arrives in ports already frozen, packaged, and destined for specific markets by contract. You are indeed lucky if you live in or near a coastal town where commercial fishing is an enterprise and you can get your fish and shellfish fresh from the sea. It is truly unfortunate that in Florida, unlike in many islands of the West Indies, there is not the exciting daily event of the arrival of the fish boat when everybody gathers at the dock to make selections from the day's catch, knowing that what they buy has just come from the sea.

You may prefer to get your own, of course, deriving some sporting pleasure while at the same time you are supplying food for your table. Many people who move to Florida make fishing a way of life. You may also discover among your acquaintances a number of fishermen who catch more than they want themselves and who are happy to share with you. Some fishermen would much rather give away their catch than clean it, though this is really a simple chore once you learn how and have a bit of practice.

Seafoods are most flavorful if absolutely fresh. Much of this flavor is preserved in flash-freezing, which make many of the frozen seafoods superior to those bought presumably fresh at the market. If you do buy fish at the market, examine their eyes. They should be clear, bulging and bright. Avoid buying fish with glazed, sunken eyes. The gills should be pinkish, not gray, and the flesh should be firm. Fresh fish has only a mild fishy odor, and if the flesh is exposed, as in steaks or fillets, it will be glistening and moist rather than dried.

It is regrettable that seafoods are so little utilized in American diets. They consist largely of low-fat, low-calorie protein and are rich with vitamins and minerals. They are a primary source of iodine, essential for the proper functioning of the thyroid gland. Shrimp, oysters, and other shellfish are especially good sources of copper, iron, calcium, magnesium, and phosphorous.

It is also sadly true that a majority of Americans overcook fish. The most common method of preparing them is by frying—until they are crisp and lack most of their natural flavor. In some cases, much of the flavor has already been eliminated by the equally bad habit of soaking the fish in water for so long they become flabby. Fish and seafoods should be washed, of course, but with only exceptional cases, this should be done rapidly. Further, the fish should be dried immediately afterward. It is the natural juices of the fish that contain most of the nutrients as well as the delicate flavor. These should be retained.

The next worst way to cook fish is by boiling, which an astonishing number of people also do. This is a good way to get fish stock for some kinds of dishes, true, but in most cases this rich broth is thrown away and only the tasteless fish is eaten. Similarly, it is best in most cases not to put salt on a fish until it is time to serve it. Salt draws out the flavor. If the fish is coated with bread crumbs or filled with stuffing, the flavor will be captured, of course.

If a fish contains more than 5 percent fat, it is listed as a "fatty" fish and needs less oil or fat in cooking. Among the Florida fish in this category are mullet, pompano, and the mackerels. "Lean" fish contain less than 5 percent fat. They are firmer and generally require more oil or fat for most kinds of cooking. Drum (redfish), croakers, snapper, groupers, and bluefish are in this category.

As a rule of thumb, it is generally best to cook fish a little less than you think is necessary and also to use a moderate heat. This is another way of preserving both flavor and nutritional values. If you do fry fish, for example, do not overcook or use an exceptionally high heat. For pan frying, you can coat the fish with flour or cornmeal that you may have seasoned with thyme and some grated lime peel. The oil, shortening, or bacon grease in the frying pan should be heated before you add the fish. Turn the fish as quickly as they become brown, and cook the other side. For most fish, the cooking time will be about 5 minutes, perhaps a little longer for thicker fish but even less for thin fillets. For deep-fat frying, first coat the pieces of fish with flour or crumbs and allow the coating to dry for 20–30 minutes before cooking. Preheat the oil to 360 degrees. Immerse the pieces of fish for about 2 ½ minutes of cooking time.

Fillets, steaks, or small whole fish can be broiled. Brush them with oil and add a sprinkling of paprika and garlic powder if you like. Do not salt them. Broil one side for 5-8 minutes, depending on the sizes of the pieces of fish. Turn and broil the opposite side for slightly less time. Add salt just before serving. The pieces can also be seasoned with lime juice, melted butter, or sour cream.

For baking, the fish should be left whole—that is, only scaled and the insides removed. If you prefer, the head can also be removed. The outside of the fish should be brushed with oil, melted butter, or bacon drippings. The inside can then be filled with rice or with a bread stuffing, both of which can be variously mixed with celery, tomatoes, eggplant, mushrooms, and other combinations. The oven should be preheated to 350 degrees. Allow about 30 minutes for baking a fish that measures four inches in thickness. If you prefer to cook with a thermometer, you can remove the fish when it registers about 150 degrees on the inside.

Interestingly, over-cooking is one of the factors generating a strong, undesirable "fishy" odor.

Steaming is an excellent way of preparing fish, but this must be done carefully to assure preservation of the flavor. The fish are placed on a rack above a small amount of boiling water. The fish can be seasoned with a bit of dill, thyme, and onion and then wrapped in foil to hold in the flavor and the moisture.

On the following pages are a few recipes for various kinds of fish and shellfish generally obtainable in Florida. Do not feel obligated always to follow recipes precisely. Use them as a guide to get you started—to inspire you to create dishes that are precisely satisfying to your tastes. Like the techniques for catching fish, there is a great variety in the ways fish can be prepared. You will discover that Florida fish and shellfish are perfect companions for the fruits and vegetables of the subtropics.

Basic Baked Fish

3 lb. grouper, snapper, or other lean fish
4-6 slices of onion
1 tbsp. soy sauce
1 tsp. salt
½ tsp. pepper
½ cup melted butter
½ tsp. thyme
4 tbsp. lime juice (or orange juice)

Put fish in greased pan. Insert slices of onion into cuts made at 2-inch intervals along sides of fish. Mix other ingredients with the melted butter and coat the fish inside and out. Use remainder to baste the fish during the cooking process. Bake in oven preheated to 350 degrees until fish flakes easily. That will require about 30 minutes. Serves 3-4.

Vinegar variation: Rub fish inside and out with vinegar before baking. Cut slits in sides of fish (as above) but insert pieces of bacon (slices cut in halves or thirds). Bake as described above.

Stuffed Fish

  3 lb. fish, grouper, snapper, or other lean fish
  1 medium-sized onion, diced
  1 ½ cups bread stuffing
  1 tbsp. lime juice
  1 tsp. salt
  ¼ cup melted butter
  3-4 tomatoes, sliced
  2 slices of bacon
  1 medium-sized onion, sliced
  ¼ tsp. pepper

Mix bread crumbs, diced onion, salt, pepper and lime juice; spoon this mixture into cavity of fish. Bake for about 30 minutes at 350 degrees. Meanwhile, cook the bacon slowly in frying pan until it is done but not crisp. Place slices of bacon, tomato, and onion on the fish and return it to the oven for an additional 10 minutes. Serves 3-4.

Fish Stuffed with Oysters

  3 lb. fish, grouper, snapper, or other lean fish
  ⅓ cup melted butter
  1 cup dry white wine
  1 stalk of celery, including top
  2-3 tomatoes, sliced
  1 ½ cups bread crumbs
  1 tbsp. lime juice
  1 large onion, sliced and separated into rings
  1 doz. oysters
  1 tsp. salt
  ¼ tsp. pepper

Pour butter and wine into baking dish. Make a layer of celery, including tops, in bottom of pan. Add a layer of onion rings on top of celery, then a layer of slices of tomatoes. Fill cavity of fish with buttered mixture of bread crumbs, oysters (whole or chopped), tomatoes, and remaining onions. Pour lime juice over the mixture and season with salt and pepper. If desired, several drops of Tabasco sauce and a sprinkling of paprika can be added. Bake for about 30 minutes at 350 degrees, basting frequently. Serves 4-6.

Mushroom-Rice Stuffing

Prepare fish as above but stuff with a mixture of precooked rice

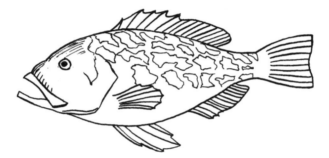

and mushrooms, seasoned with finely chopped celery, diced onions, thyme, salt and pepper.

Shrimp Stuffing

> 2 cups cooked shrimp, ground or finely chopped
> 2 eggs, lightly beaten
> ½ cup cream
> ⅛ tsp. pepper
> 1 can (4 oz.) mushrooms
> ¼ cup dry white wine
> 1 tsp. salt
> ¼ tsp. paprika

Mix eggs, shrimp, mushrooms, wine, and seasonings with cream and stir briskly to make a thick paste. Spread this mixture between two fillets of fish, such as pompano, which is then placed in oven and baked.

Sour Cream Stuffing (for about 3 lb. fish)

¾ cup sour cream
¾ cup onion, chopped
1 cup celery, chopped
3 cups bread crumbs
1 tbsp. lime juice
¼ tsp. pepper
3 tbsp. melted butter or olive oil
1 tsp. paprika
1 tsp. thyme
1 tsp. salt

Saute celery and onions in oil or butter until tender, then add sour cream, bread crumbs, lime juice, and seasonings. Mix thoroughly. Stuff fish after it has baked for about 30 minutes. Return to oven for additional 10 minutes.

Milk-and-Bread Stuffing

2 tbsp. melted butter or oil
1 medium-sized onion, finely chopped
2 cups bread stuffing
¼ cup milk
1 egg, lightly beaten
¾ cup chopped celery
1 tsp. salt
¼ tsp. sage
⅛ tsp. pepper

Brown onions in the butter or oil. Soak the bread in milk and then pour mixture over the onions. Add egg, celery, salt, pepper, and sage. Mix thoroughly. Stuff fish after it has baked for about 30 minutes. Return stuffed fish to oven for additional 10 minutes.

Martinique Baked Fish

3 lbs. pompano, snapper, grouper, or comparable fish
1 large onion, chopped
¾ cup mushrooms
1 cup dry white wine
4 tomatoes, chopped
½ cup bread crumbs
1 bay leaf
¼ tsp. thyme
1 tsp. chopped parsley
¼ cup butter
2 tbsp. flour
½ tsp. salt
¼ tsp. pepper

Put chopped onions, parsley, thyme, and bay leaf (break in 2-3 pieces) in bottom of greased baking pan. Place fish on top of seasonings and pour wine over fish and herbs. Bake for about 25 minutes at 350 degrees. Melt butter in frying pan and add flour, stirring until brown. Add mushrooms and tomatoes, cooking for 15-20 minutes on a low heat. Spoon this mixture over the fish, top with bread crumbs, and bake for additional 10 minutes. Serves 4-6.

Cucumber Stuffing for Baked Fish

5 tbsp. diced cucumber
2 tbsp. green pepper, chopped
2 tbsp. parsley, chopped
½ tsp. grated lime rind
3 tbsp. minced onion
1 cup bread crumbs
6 tbsp. melted butter
⅛ tsp. thyme
⅛ tsp. sage
½ tsp. salt

⅛ tsp. pepper
¼ cup water

Combine the above ingredients and mix thoroughly. This is enough to make a stuffing for a fish weighing 3-5 lbs.

Baked Fillets and Steaks

Fillets and steaks can be baked in the same manner as whole fish but because they are thinner and the flesh more exposed, the time required for baking is about a third less. A stuffing can be placed between two fillets, or a single fillet can be rolled and held together with toothpicks, forming a cavity that can be stuffed.

Almond Sauce

Chopped almonds browned in butter and then seasoned with lime juice, salt, and pepper makes an excellent sauce for baked fillets.

Mullet in Lime Sauce

Mullet is a fatty fish that is a favorite of native Floridians. A popular way of preparing it is by baking the fillets and pouring over the top a sauce consisting of ¼ cup of butter, 1 tbsp. lime juice, 1 small onion finely chopped, 1 tsp. salt, and ⅛ tsp. pepper. Flavor of the mullet can be preserved by wrapping fillets and seasoning in foil during the baking. Foil can be opened and fish browned under broiler just before serving, if desired.

Baked Fillets with Potatoes

3 lbs. fillets of snapper or comparable fish
1 large onion, chopped
1 tbsp. parsley, chopped
2 tbsp. butter
¼ tsp. thyme
¼ tsp. marjoram
⅛ tsp. pepper

1 lime
5-6 medium-sized potatoes, boiled
1 green pepper, chopped
¼ tsp. dried, hot peppers (optional)
1 tsp. salt
¼ tsp. paprika

Place fillets in baking dish and pour over them ¼ cup olive oil and juice from ½ lime. Cover fish with chopped onions. Add marjoram, thyme, dried hot peppers, salt and pepper. Bake for about 30 minutes at 350 degrees. Saute green peppers until tender. Cut boiled potatoes into wedges and add to frying pan, cooking until browned. Place cooked fish in center of platter and arrange the cooked peppers and potatoes around the edge. Pour melted butter over both fish and potatoes just before serving. Serves 4-6.

Baked Fillets, Caribbean Style

3 lbs. fillets of snappers or comparable fish
2 large onions, sliced
1 clove garlic, crushed
3 medium-sized tomatoes, sliced
1 dozen black olives
1 tbsp. capers
1 cup olive oil
1 cup white wine
1 green pepper, diced
1 lime
1 tsp. salt
½ tsp. pepper
½ tsp. thyme
1 bay leaf
¼ tsp. fresh ginger

Place fillets in baking dish and squeeze juice of lime over them. Salt and pepper the fillets, then pour over them ½ cup of oil and the cup of wine. Cover fillets with slices of onions. Add bay leaf and sprinkle with the thyme and ginger. Bake in oven at 350 degrees for about 30 minutes.

Saute garlic in remaining oil. Add tomatoes and the remaining onions. In about 3 minutes add green peppers, capers, and olives. Simmer until mixture begins to thicken. Add the baked fillets and allow to simmer for additional 5 minutes before serving. Serves 3-4.

Fried Fish with Green Bean Sauce

2 lbs of fillets of mackerel, seatrout, mullet, or comparable fish
1 cup olive oil
1 clove garlic, crushed
½ cup flour
1 tsp. salt
⅛ tsp. pepper
½ cup green beans
dash of cayenne pepper

Add crushed garlic to juice of lime and spread over fillets. Allow to marinate for at least 2 hours. Dry fillets and cover with flour. Fry them in oil until brown. Cover with sauce made of lime juice, cayenne pepper, salt, pepper, and chopped onions mixed thoroughly with the cooked green beans. In the sauce, vinegar can be substituted for the lime juice if desired. Serves 3-4.

Fried Fish with Lime-Tomato Sauce

2 lbs. fillets of mullet, mackerel, seatrout, or comparable fish
1 cup olive oil
½ cup lime juice
½ cup tomato sauce
4 tbsp. flour
1 ½ cups water
1 tsp. thyme
1 tsp. sugar
3 cloves garlic, crushed

1 tsp. salt
¼ tsp. pepper
1 tsp. rosemary

Coat fish with lime juice and sprinkle with pepper. Dip pieces of fish in flour and fry in small amount of oil until golden brown. Pour oil from pan and strain it. Wipe pan clean with paper towel. Pour 1 cup of oil into pan, adding additional oil if too much was used in the frying. Add the flour, stirring with a spoon until the heated oil and flour mixture becomes light brown. Add lime juice, water, tomato sauce, sugar, salt, pepper, and garlic. Stir mixture until it is smooth. Simmer for about 20 minutes. Pour this sauce over the fish in baking dish and place in oven at 300 degrees for about 10 minutes. Allow to cool. This dish can be eaten while still warm or when it becomes cold. Serves 3-4.

Fish and Rice

3 lbs. of grouper, snapper, or comparable fish, cut into chunks
4 large onions, quartered or cut into slices
1 ½ cups of rice
1 tsp. salt
½ tsp. pepper
1 cup olive oil
⅛ tsp. saffron

Fry chunks of fish in oil until brown. In separate pan, saute onions until they begin to turn brown. Place onions in large saucepan, adding saffron, salt, pepper and about ½ cup of water. Add the fish, adding more water to cover. Bring contents to boil, then add rice and additional water (about 1 cup). As water cooks away from surface of fish and rice, add more water to keep the contents covered. Reduce heat to medium-low. When water is again low, check to see if rice is done. If not, add more water; continue cooking. Serve as soon as rice is ready. Serves 4-6.

Fish in Coconut Milk

   3 lbs. drum (redfish), grouper, or comparable fish
   ⅛ tsp. pepper
   1 coconut
   1 lime
   ½ cup cooking oil
   1 tsp. salt
   1 clove of garlic, crushed
   2 medium-sized onions

Cover fish with lime juice, mixed with pepper, chopped onion, and crushed garlic. Allow to stand in covered dish for half an hour or longer. Heat oil in frying pan and add the onions and other seasonings, removing them from fish. Add milk from coconut. Put fish in pan and cook at medium heat, basting frequently until fish is thoroughly cooked. This will require about 30 minutes. Serve on a platter, covering fish with a sauce made by blending 1 cup of coconut milk with 2 tbsp. butter, 2 tbsp. flour, salt and pepper. Sauce should be heated before pouring it over the fish. Most desirable, the sauce and fish can be heated together if the fish is served on a metal platter. Serves 3-4

   Note: Coconut milk is obtained by putting diced coconut meat in bag, pouring hot water (as many cups of hot water as there are cups of coconut meat) over the coconut, and squeezing out the milky fluid. It is not the "water" from inside the coconut.

Grouper Parmesan

   2-2 ½ lbs of grouper fillets (or comparable fish)
   1 cup sour cream
   ¼ cup Parmesan cheese, grated
   1 tbsp. lime juice
   1 tbsp. fresh parsley, chopped
   1 small onion, finely diced
   ½ tsp. salt
   ¼ tsp. black pepper

paprika
Tabasco sauce

Cut fillets into serving size pieces and place in a single layer in a greased baking dish. Combine the sour cream, cheese, onion, and seasonings, including 2-3 drops of Tabasco, and spread this mixture over the top of the fillets. Sprinkle with paprika. Place in oven at 350 degrees for about 30 minutes or less, checking to see if fish flakes easily with fork. Garnish with the parsley. Serves 4.

Broiled Dilled Fish

2 ½-3 lbs. fillets of mackerel, snapper, grouper, or comparable fish
1 medium-sized onion, chopped
1 sprig of fresh dill (or 2 tsp. dill seed)
1 tsp. pepper (freshly ground best)
1 cup wine vinegar
⅓ cup butter

Use only large fillets, placing them in a greased baking dish and then sprinkling with dill, salt, pepper, and onions. Pour vinegar over the top and marinate overnight. Remove fillets from marinade and place in broiler pan or on aluminum foil. Broil 5-8 minutes, then turn and broil other side for slightly less time. Pour any liquids into the baking pan, which still contains the marinade. Add butter to marinade, then heat and pour over the fish as a sauce. Serves 3-4.

Broiled Fish Steaks

3 lbs. snapper or mackerel steaks or small fillets
¼ tsp. pepper
1 tbsp. chili sauce
1 tbsp. horseradish
1 tbsp. catsup
1 tbsp. prepared mustard
1 cup grated cheddar cheese
1 tsp. salt

Brush fish with oil or butter and broil, about 3 inches from heat, for 6–8 minutes on one side, then turn fish, coat the other side, and broil for about 5 minutes. If fillets are large, cut slices about 2 inches apart to prevent curling as fish cooks. Mix mustard, catsup, chili sauce, and horseradish and spread over the fish, at the same time adding salt and pepper. Sprinkle cheese over the top of the fish and return fish to broiler until cheese melts and begins to turn toasty brown. Serves 3-4.

For a variation, marinate fillets for several hours in French dressing before broiling. For a sauce, mix 1 small, minced onion, ½ tsp. prepared mustard, salt, pepper, and paprika with a cup of sour cream.

Spicy Broiled Fillets

    3 lbs. fillet of snappers, grouper, or other fish
    3 tbsp. horseradish
    1 tsp. salt
    ¾ cup chili sauce
    ½ cup prepared mustard
    2 tbsp. Worcestershire sauce
    ¼ tsp. pepper

Put fillets in greased broiler pan or on foil. Mix other ingredients and spread over the fish. Broil for 8–10 minutes on one side, then turn and broil for about 5 minutes on other side. Serves 3-4.

Florida Fish Cutlets

    3 lbs. mullet, snapper, or other fish fillets
    2 limes
    ¼ lb. butter or margarine
    ½ cup bread crumbs
    1 tsp. salt
    ¼ tsp. pepper
    2 eggs, beaten lightly

Squeeze lime juice over fish and allow to marinate for at least an hour. The lime juice breaks down the connective tissues in the fish, thus tenderizing it. Add salt and pepper to bread crumbs. Heat butter in frying pan. Dip pieces of fish into egg and then into crumbs. Fry until golden brown on one side, then turn and fry other side. Serves 3-4.

Jamaican Grilled Fish

3-4 lbs. fillets of snapper or other fish
1 tbsp. olive oil
1 ½ cups vinegar
4 medium-sized onions, sliced
2 bay leaves
2 tsp. salt
½ tsp. pepper
3 medium-sized carrots, cut in lengthwise pieces about 2 inches long
3 large green peppers, chopped or in slices

Brush fillets with oil and broil, turning as soon as brown on one side and then browning the other. Depending on thickness of fillets, this will require 8-10 minutes for first side, and 5-8 minutes for remaining side. Put peppers, onions, carrots, bay leaves, vinegar, olive oil, salt, and pepper in saucepan. Mix well and then bring to a boil. Allow to simmer for 20-30 minutes. Pour heated, blended sauce over the broiled fillets. Serves 4-6.

Fish Pancakes

2-3 lbs. of fillets of grunts or other small fish
2 tbsp. flour
1 clove of garlic, crushed
1 tsp. salt
⅛ tsp. pepper
2 eggs, lightly beaten
¼ tsp. thyme (optional)

Put fillets in blender and pulverize at high speed. It will be necessary to add a small amount of water to get blender to operate properly, and it may be necessary also to do the fish in small amounts, repeating the process until all of the fish have been through the blender. Add the flour, eggs, and seasonings to the fish. Mix thoroughly. Spoon this mixture in small pancake sized portions onto a hot, greased griddle or into frying pan. Use spatula to press them thin. Cook until golden brown on one side, then turn and brown other side. Excellent when served with a green salad. This is also a superb way of using smaller fish that might otherwise be wasted. Serves 3-4.

Fillets Fried in Milk

> 2-3 lbs. of snapper fillets or other fish
> 1 cup flour
> 1 tsp. salt
> ¼ tsp. pepper
> 1 cup milk

Add salt and pepper to milk. Dip fillets in milk, then in flour. Fry either in deep fat or in a skillet. Do not cook fish for more than 3 minutes on each side. Place pieces on paper towels to absorb oil before putting them on platter. Serves 3-4.

Spicy Sauce for Fried Fish

> 1 tbsp. mustard
> 2 tsp. horseradish
> ¾ cup creamy salad dressing
> 2-3 drops Tabasco sauce
> ½ tsp. salt
> ⅛ tsp. pepper
> 1 tsp. sweet pickle relish

Mix ingredients until smooth and use as a cold sauce for fried fish.

Fish Chowder

> 2 lbs. fish fillets
> 3 slices of bacon (or salt pork)

1 cup of chopped onion
2 tsp. salt
⅛ tsp. thyme
2 cups of diced or thinly sliced potatoes
4 cups homogenized milk
¼ tsp. pepper
⅛ tsp. paprika

Fry bacon until crisp, then remove pieces of bacon from frying pan. Add onions to frying pan and brown, using moderate heat. Add potatoes and cover with water. Cook until tender. Cut fish fillets into 1 ½-inch chunks and mix with potatoes, cooking until fish flakes easily with a fork. Add fish and potatoes to milk in larger pan, seasoning with the salt, pepper, thyme and paprika. Heat thoroughly but do not boil. Stir to mix ingredients and spread seasoning throughout the chowder. Serve while steaming hot. Excellent way of utilizing sheepshead and grouper. Serves 3–4.

Fish Flakes

Cook fish in salted water until fish flakes. Remove fish from water and use a fork to flake all of the cooked fish from the bones. The flaked fish can then be used in casseroles—with potatoes, ham, macaroni, cheese—the combinations are almost infinite. Cold, flaked fish can also be added to tossed salads, cucumber salads, or potato salads. Mixed with a bit of lime juice, chopped celery, mayonnaise, mustard, salt, and pepper, they make an excellent sandwich spread.

SHELLFISH

Oysters

To many people, oysters are the favorite of all the seafoods, and they are surprised to find that Florida offers some of the finest to be had, harvested either from natural beds or produced on "sea farms." The most productive areas commercially are near Apalachicola in the Florida panhandle and in the Crystal River area midway on the West Coast. Natural oyster beds can still be found in many areas, from the panhandle through the Keys. One of the delights of a Florida outing is harvesting oysters and then eating them soon afterward—raw, baked, or turned into a stew. If you buy oysters in the shell, make certain they are still alive. If they are, their shells will be tightly shut, or the oyster will snap its shell shut as soon as you begin handling it.

OYSTERS ON THE HALF SHELL

Shuck as many oysters as will be needed for the number of persons you expect to serve. About half a dozen oysters per person is generally sufficient. If you have never shucked oysters, it might be best to have this done at the market. Shucking is fast and easy only after you have some experience. The washed oyster shell is held in the left hand with the flat side of the shell up. The other side is pressed firmly against a bench or table. An oyster knife, which has a short, stout blade and a sturdy handle, is then forced between the shells at the tip end. Often it is necessary to break off the tip of the shell with a hammer so that it is easy to insert the knife. Slide the knife along the top of the flat shell to cut the big muscle that holds the oyster in its shell. As the shell is lifted away, continue to sever the muscle attachments. The oyster will be left in the deep, cupped half of the shell. The flat portion is thrown away.

Sauces for oysters on the half shell consist of various mixtures of catsup with lime juice and seasoning. For a starter or a guide, try this one:

½ cup catsup, 2 tbsp. horseradish, 1 tbsp. finely chopped onion, 2 tbsp. lime juice, 2 tbsp. finely chopped celery (or 1 tsp. celery salt), 1 tsp. Worcestershire sauce, 1 ½ tsp. soy sauce—mixed thoroughly and chilled before serving.

Oysters Baked in Shells

> 6-8 oysters per person
> 1 medium-sized onion, diced
> butter
> paprika
> salt
> pepper
> thyme, or marjoram

Leave shucked oysters in shells. Season with diced onions, salt, pepper, and paprika, adding thyme or marjoram if desired. Put a dot of butter on each oyster. Bake in oven at 375 degrees for about 10 minutes.

Broiled Marinated Oysters

> 6-8 oysters for each serving
> ½ slice of bacon for each oyster
> ¼ cup sherry wine
> ½ cup melted butter or oil
> chopped parsley
> salt
> pepper
> 1 tsp. Worcestershire sauce

Marinate oysters in mixture of wine, butter (or oil), and seasonings. Wrap each oyster in half a slice of bacon and broil until bacon is cooked. Be sure oysters are covered completely with bacon as they require less cooking time.

Limed Oysters

6-8 oysters per serving
½ cup butter
½ cup flour
¼ cup lime juice
Tabasco sauce
salt
pepper

Roll oysters in flour and then brown them in butter. Hold in heated pan or on serving platter. Brown remaining flour in butter. Add 3-4 drops of Tabasco, plus the salt and pepper. Heat until mixture begins to bubble. Pour over oysters and serve.

For serving, the shucked oysters can be arranged on a bed of ice in bowls or deep plates. A typical and attractive arrangement consists of six oysters in a circle with a bowl of sauce in the center.

Pickled Oysters

1 qt. oysters
4-6 whole allspice
4-6 whole cloves
⅛ tsp. cayenne pepper
1 cup vinegar (white preferred)
½ tsp. mace
salt

Put oysters in pan and pour vinegar over them. Add seasonings. Heat, stopping when oysters have become plump and edges begin to curl. Allow to cool. Serve pickled oysters on lettuce as a main course or as a salad companion to a meal of some other seafood. Serves 3-4.

Fried Oysters

2-3 doz. oysters
2 eggs, lightly beaten
⅛ tsp. pepper
1 cup bread crumbs
1 tsp. salt

Beat eggs, adding seasoning and small amounts of water. Dip oysters one at a time into mixture, then into crumbs. Let stand for about 5 minutes before cooking. Fry in cooking oil at about 375 degrees. Serves 3-4.

Broiled Oysters on Toast

2 doz. or more oysters (6-8 per serving)
8 slices of toast, buttered (or allow 1 slice per 3 oysters)
2 limes
1 cup butter, melted
½ tsp. salt
⅛ tsp. cayenne
½ cup bread crumbs
sprigs of parsley for garnish

Dip oysters first in melted butter, seasoned with salt and cayenne, and then into bread crumbs. Broil until brown. Add lime juice to butter and pour over oysters. Put about 3 oysters on each slice of toast. Garnish with parsley.

Scalloped Oysters

1 qt. oysters
1 cup butter, melted
½ tsp. Worcestershire sauce
2 cups milk
4 cups cracker crumbs
1 tsp. salt
¼ tsp. pepper
¼ cup cheddar cheese

Combine cracker crumbs with Worcestershire sauce, salt, pepper, and butter. Put about a third of this mixture in the bottom of a casserole dish that has been greased with butter. Add layer of oysters. Put layer of cracker crumbs over the top, then another layer of oysters, topping with the remaining crumbs. Add the milk. Bake at 350 degrees for about 30 minutes. Top with grated cheese, returning to oven only long enough to melt the cheese. Serves 3-4.

Variations in preparing scalloped oysters are numerous. As one example, a can of condensed celery soup can be substituted for the milk. Seasoning can include chopped parsley, some chopped onion, and a tsp. of dry mustard. Or 1-2 eggs, lightly beaten, can be added to the milk before it is poured into casserole. Once the basics are mastered, the creative cook can season to suit his taste.

Oyster Stew

1 qt. oysters
½ cup butter
2 tsp. salt
½ tsp. pepper
2 quarts milk

Cook oysters in butter until edges curl. Add milk, salt, and pepper. Heat but do not boil. Stew can be garnished with parsley or sprinkled with paprika when served. Serves 4-6.

Variations are many. For example, inside of saucepan can be rubbed with garlic before cooking. A few drops of Tabasco sauce or a bit of Worcestershire sauce can be added if desired to spice the stew.

Barbecued Oysters

1 qt. oysters
1 cup chili sauce
½ cup water
1 medium-sized onion, diced
½ cup lime juice

¼ cup melted butter
¼ cup brown sugar
¼ tsp. Tabasco sauce
1 tbsp. prepared mustard
3 tsp. salt
½ tsp. pepper

Mix all ingredients, except oysters, in a saucepan and simmer to make sauce. Spread oysters on broiler pan or on foil and cook until brown. Pour sauce over oysters or dip them. Serves 3-4.

Oyster Stuffing

1 pt. oysters
½ cup butter, melted
4 cups of bread crumbs or stuffing
1 tbsp. lime juice
2 tsp. salt
¼ tsp. pepper

Combine all ingredients and use as a stuffing for chicken or turkey.

SCALLOPS

Like oysters, scallops are bivalved mollusks, but they do not grow attached in one spot. In scallops, only the large muscle that closes the shell is eaten. As a rule, scallops are bought already shucked and, most commonly, frozen. The price paid for scallops may seem high, but all of the meat is edible. In Florida, some people prefer to harvest their own scallops which are sometimes abundant in inshore waters. These scallops are small and pinkish. The meat of those taken from deeper, offshore waters is white. Because the meat is tough, the larger ones are generally scored with a knife.

Scallops are most commonly fried in butter and seasoned with salt and pepper. They can actually be substituted for oysters in all of the recipes in which oysters are cooked.

Deviled Scallops

1 lb. scallops
¼ cup bread crumbs
1 tsp. parsley, chopped
2-3 drops of Tabasco
3 tbsp. butter
1 tbsp. prepared mustard
½ tsp. salt
1 small onion, finely diced

Put scallops in ½ cup of water and heat to boiling. Drain off liquid and save. Cut cooked scallops into small chunks. Mix butter, mustard, and seasonings, with liquid drained from scallops. Pour this over the scallops and allow to marinate for an hour or longer. Place in baking dish, cover top with bread crumbs, and bake for about 30 minutes at 350 degrees. Serves 3-4.

Scallop Salad

1 pt. scallops
1 small onion, diced
1 clove garlic, minced or crushed
¼ cup sweet pickle relish, or diced sweet pickles
1 cup celery, chopped
¼ cup mayonnaise or other creamy salad dressing
½ cup French dressing
1 tsp. salt
⅛ tsp. pepper

Cook scallops in boiling, salted water for about 10 minutes. Drain, chill, and then dice. Marinate in French dressing for at least an hour. Combine all other ingredients and add to scallops. Serve either as a salad or as a main course. Serves 3.

Baked Scallops

 1 pt. scallops
 2 hardcooked eggs, diced
 1 tsp. lime juice
 ½ tsp. prepared mustard
 ¼ tsp. salt
 Parmesan cheese
 ½ cup bread crumbs
 1 tbsp. green pepper finely chopped
 1 can cream of mushroom soup
 ⅛ tsp. pepper

Thin mushroom soup with 1 can of water, then add all other ingredients and mix. Put mixture in baking dish or in scallop shells (if these have been saved and scrubbed). Cover with bread crumbs and sprinkle with Parmesan cheese. Bake at 400 degrees for about 20 minutes. Serves 3-4.

Scalloped Scallops

 1 ½ lbs. scallops
 1 ½ cups cracker crumbs
 ½ cup butter, melted
 1 tbsp. lime juice
 1 tsp. salt
 1 small onion, finely diced or minced
 ⅛ tsp. pepper

Cut scallops in half or in quarters, depending on size. Add other ingredients to melted butter and mix thoroughly. Place layer of scallops in greased baking dish, then top with seasoning mixture. Add another layer of scallops, then seasoning, etc. until all are used. Bake at 400 degrees for about 20 minutes. Serves 3-4.

CLAMS

Though they are not as popular in Florida as are oysters, clams are an abundantly available seafood along many Florida coastal areas. Of the edible species, the largest is the surf clam, its shell as much as 6 inches long. Nearly as large and often weighing several pounds is the hard-shelled clam, best known farther north as the quahog or little-necked clam. It was the shells of this clam that were converted into wampum and used as money by the Indians.

Like oysters, clams can be eaten raw on the half shell. If they are bought in the shell, check to make certain they are still alive, as with oysters. If the clams have already been shucked, the meats should be plump and in a reasonably clear liquid, with few or no pieces of shells. Clams can also be bought canned or frozen.

Most large clams are tough but can be made manageable by mincing or chopping them before they are cooked.

If you harvest the clams yourself, wash them several times in fresh water to get rid of the sand. To whiten them and also to make it unnecessary to clean out their stomachs when the shells are finally opened, put the clams in a bucket or a tub and cover them with water to which you have added a cup of cornmeal for each gallon of clams. Allow them to stand in this water for at least 6 hours—longer if you have a lot of clams. Wash the clams thoroughly and then cover them again with water. The shells will open slightly. Insert a stout, thick-bladed knife (oyster knife if you have one) and run it around the shell, cutting the muscle that holds the shell shut and at the same time prying open the shell. If you intend to serve the clams on the half shell, remove only half of the shell.

French Fried Clams

1 qt. of shucked clams
2 tbsp. milk

1 ½ tsp. salt
⅛ tsp. pepper
2 eggs, lightly beaten
2 cups of bread or cracker crumbs
½ cup cooking oil

Mix the eggs, milk, and seasonings. Drain claims and dip them one at a time first into the mixture of eggs and milk and then into the bread crumbs. Fry in cooking oil at 375 degrees for about 5 minutes on one side and then turning to cook the other side for about 3 minutes. Serves 3-4.

Clam Fritters

1 qt. clams
¼ lb. diced bacon, or salt pork
2 tbsp. flour
⅛ lb. butter
¼ tsp. pepper
1 cup celery, chopped
4 medium-sized onions, diced
4 potatoes, diced
1 ½ quarts milk
1 tsp. salt

Grind or chop clams and heat in their juice. Fry bacon until crisp. Remove pieces of bacon from pan and save. Saute onions and celery in bacon fat. Sprinkle potatoes with flour and add to onions and celery. Cook until potatoes are tender. Put clams, crisp bacon pieces, and the potatoes, onions, and celery in deep pan with warmed milk. Dot the top with butter. Serve when the butter melts. Serves 4-6.

Clams on the Half Shell

6-8 clams per person
sauce

As with oysters, arrange clams on a bed of crushed ice in a bowl or deep plate, with a small dish of cocktail sauce in the center. Parsley makes an attractive garnish. Add a wedge of lime for individual use. Sauce can be the same as for oysters.

Deviled Clams

1 qt. clams, chopped
1 egg, lightly beaten
2 tomatoes, chopped
2 tsp. salt
¼ cup melted butter
¼ cup cracker crumbs
2 medium onions, diced
1 small green pepper, chopped
1 stalk celery, finely chopped
½ tsp. pepper
1 tsp. prepared mustard

Saute onions until brown. Add clams, tomatoes, green pepper, celery, pepper, salt, mustard, cracker crumbs, and a small amount of water for moistening fluid. Mix thoroughly and simmer for 3-5 minutes. Allow to cool slightly. Fill clam shells with this mixture and bake them in oven at 350 degrees for about 20 minutes. Remove and sprinkle with Parmesan cheese. Return to oven until cheese melts. Serves 4-6.

Steamed Clams

6-8 clams per person
melted butter, or cocktail sauce

Put thoroughly washed clams in steamer with about 1 cup of water. Steam until clams open—in 5-10 minutes. Serve in the shells, with either melted butter or cocktail sauce.

COQUINAS

These tiny clams of the genus Donox are unbelievably abundant at times on some of Florida's sand beaches. As the waves recede, the sand seems to be literally alive as the tiny little clams squirm deeper into the sand to wait for the next wave to roll in. A handful of sand may contain two or three dozen of the colorful little shells, none of which measure more than half an inch long. When coquinas are at a population peak, a quart or more can be collected in only a few minutes.

For eating, wash the coquinas several times in cold water. Put them in a kettle, cover them with water, and heat to boiling. After about 5 minutes, stir vigorously to loosen some of the little clams from their now-open shells. Strain off the coquina broth and as many clams as you can. Add salt and pepper to taste and float a patty of butter in each bowl of the hot, delicately flavored broth.

CONCHS

These large snails gave the natives of the Florida Keys their familiar nickname—"conks," which is also the way to pronounce conch. Removing a conch from its shell is easy after you are experienced but may seem absolutely impossible without guidance. Old timers break off the tip of the shell, slip the blade of a knife inside, and cut loose the muscle that holds the snail inside. They do this so fast that it seems to be no chore at all. If you want to save the shell, you may be able to force the conch to come out by coating its exposed portions with salt, then grabbing it firmly and pulling. Or you can boil the conch in its shell.

Conchs are extremely tough and require long cooking to soften them. They can also be eaten raw, like oysters, but should be marinated first in lime juice to tenderize them a bit. Conch meat cut into bite-sized pieces makes an excellent addition to a tossed salad, turning it into a main course. Conchs can also be used in a variety of other ways, some of which are noted here.

A favorite seasoning for conchs in the Bahamas, the West Indies, and among Florida old timers is "old sour." This is made by dissolving a tablespoon of salt in a pint of lime juice, which is then allowed to ferment at room temperature for at least two weeks before it is used. If it is preferred spicy hot, a dash of cayenne pepper can be added to the brew. Old sour is used not only on conchs but also on other seafoods and meats, both as a condiment and as a marinade.

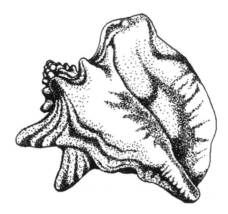

conch salad

2 conchs, ground or chopped

3 limes, juiced

½ tsp. oregano

1 tsp. salt

½ cup olive oil

2 avocados

1 green pepper, chopped

1 medium-sized onion, chopped

1 clove of garlic

1 tsp. chopped parsley

1 tbsp. vinegar

⅛ tsp. curry

2-3 drops Tabasco

Put conchs and all ingredients except avocados in a bowl. Mix and then allow to marinate for at least 8 hours. Cut avocados in half, remove seeds and fill cavity with conch mixture. Can be used as an appetizer, salad, or main course. Serves 4.

Conch Chowder

1 lb. of conch meat
1 large onion, diced
1 stalk celery, chopped
2 cans tomato paste
1 tsp. salt
4 cooked potatoes, diced
¼ cup lime juice
1 clove garlic, crushed
4 tbsp. cooking oil
4 qts. water
¼ tsp. pepper

Cook conchs in boiling water, then cut into bite-sized pieces. Marinate conch meat in lime juice for about 4 hours. Brown the onions, garlic, and celery in cooking oil. Add tomato paste and simmer for 10-15 minutes. Add water, salt, and pepper. Bring mixture to a boil and add potatoes. Continue to cook until the potatoes are nearly done. Add the conch and continue slow cooking for a brief time, stirring occasionally to mix seasonings. As soon as potatoes are cooked, chowder is ready to serve. Serves 4-6.

SHRIMP

Floridians living in some coastal areas are fortunate in being able to get fresh-caught shrimp, but most of the commercial catch is processed aboard the fishing vessels and arrives in port already frozen and contracted for. Shrimp are graded by size, which varies with the species as well as with individuals, from small (more than 42 to the pound) through mediums and large to jumbos (fewer than 25 to the pound). Among these are the large royal reds caught off the Dry Tortugas and also off northeastern Florida. Their flavor is between that of the usual pink, brown, or white shrimp and a lobster.

Shrimp can be served as a main course, in salads, or as a major component of a variety of dishes.

Boiled Shrimp with Peels On

> 3 lbs. of shrimp
> 2 limes, sliced
> 2 ½-3 qts. water
> ¼ cup salt

Wash shrimp thoroughly. Boil water, to which the salt and lime slices have been added. Put shrimp in water, cover, and bring water to boil again. Allow to simmer for about 5 minutes, or until shells of shrimp turn pink. Pour off water and cool the shrimp. Break up front section of body and then peel tail meat from shell. Pull sand vein from groove along back, if necessary cutting a slit with knife to make removal of vein easier. Serves 3-4.

Seasoning can be varied greatly in this initial boiling of shrimp. Commercial shrimp-boil spices are available, or you can do the seasoning to suit your taste. Try 2 cups of diced celery, a medium sized chopped onion, a bay leaf, a dozen or so peppercorns, 2 tsp. thyme, and a tsp. of caraway seeds. Simmer these ingredients for 20-30 minutes before adding the shrimp.

Cocktail Sauces for Shrimp

Variations in cocktail sauces for shrimp are virtually limitless. Here are some starters:

Combine ½ cup of salad oil with ¼ cup vinegar, 1 tbsp. horse-radish, 1 tbsp. prepared mustard, ½ tsp. pepper, 1 tsp. salt, ½ tsp. celery seed, 2-3 drops of Tabasco, and 1 tbsp. paprika. This is deliciously spicy and different.

Another can be made by using 1 cup of catsup as the base, adding 1 tbsp. horseradish, 2 tbsp. vinegar, 1 tbsp. of finely diced celery, ½ tsp. salt, 2-3 drops of Tabasco, and 1 tsp. of Worcestershire sauce.

Another type, also popular for freshly cooked shrimp, is made by mixing 1 cup of chopped celery with ½ cup of French dressing, and 1 cup of mayonnaise, seasoning with 1 tsp. salt, ½ tsp. pepper, and ½ tsp. dry mustard.

Shrimp with Pineapple, Avocado, and Orange

  2 cups cooked shrimp
  1 orange
  1 avocado
  1 large pineapple
  1 grapefruit
  1 lime

Cut pineapple in half lengthwise and remove core and meat from each half. Peel orange and grapefruit and section. Peel avocado and dice, sprinkling with lime juice. Fill the two pineapple halves with a mixture of orange, grapefruit, and avocado. Place chilled shrimp on top. Make a dressing consisting of 1 tsp. honey, ½ tsp. salt, ½ tsp. paprika, ½ cup salad oil, 2 tbsp. of dry, white wine, and 2 tbsp. lime juice. Pour over the top of shrimp. Serves 3-4.

Peppers Stuffed with Shrimp

  2 cups cooked shrimp
  1 tbsp. chopped onion
  1 tsp. salt
  ⅛ tsp. pepper
  2 tbsp. butter
  4 large green peppers
  1 cup bread crumbs
  1 stewed tomato
  ¼ tsp. oregano

Cut tops off pepper. Dice usable portions of top to add to other ingredients. Remove cores and seeds from peppers and wash hollow cavities. Parboil peppers until tender. Saute onions and peppers, adding salt, pepper, and oregano. Add tomato and shrimp. Stuff peppers with this mixture, covering tops with bread crumbs and dotting with butter. Bake at 350 degrees for about 20 minutes, or until bread crumbs are browned. Serves 4.

Smothered Shrimp

2 ½ lbs. shrimp, shelled and deveined
1 clove garlic, crushed
2 large onions, diced
2 stalks celery, diced
2 green peppers, diced
2 tbsp. olive oil
2 tbsp. tomato paste
½ cup water
salt
pepper
Tabasco

Saute the onions, green peppers, and celery in olive oil to which the crushed garlic has been added. Reduce heat. Add water and shrimp, stirring and cooking on medium-low heat until shrimp turn pink. Stir in tomato paste. Salt and pepper to taste, adding 2-4 drops of Tabasco if you like your seafoods pepped up. Cover and continue to cook on low heat for 10 to 15 minutes. Add more water if necessary. This is excellent served on a bed of rice. Serves 4.

Fried Shrimp

3 cups cooked shrimp
½ tsp. salt
2 eggs beaten
cooking oil
2 cups flour

2 tsp. baking powder
½ cup milk

Mix flour, salt, baking powder, eggs, and milk to make a batter. Dip each shrimp into batter and make certain it is completely coated. Allow to dry. Fry coated shrimp in oil at about 375 degrees, removing when brown. Serves 3-4.

Shrimp and Okra

1 ½ lbs. of raw shrimp
3 cups of okra, sliced
2 tsp. salt
1 cup canned tomatoes
2 cups cooked rice
Tabasco sauce
3 tbsp. olive oil
1 cup chopped onion
1 clove garlic, crushed
½ tsp. pepper
1 bay leaf

Saute okra in oil, cooking about 10 minutes over medium heat. Add onions, garlic, salt, pepper, and shrimp. Stir constantly, cooking for about 5 minutes. Add 1 ½ cups of water, tomatoes, bay leaf, and 2-3 drops of Tabasco. Cover and continue cooking for about 20 minutes. Serve over rice. Serves 4-6.

Shrimp and Grapefruit

2 cups cooked shrimp
2 cups grapefruit sections
1 cup mayonnaise
1 cup diced celery

Combine above ingredients and mix thoroughly. Serve on a lettuce leaf. Serves 3-4.

Shrimp Paste

> 3 cups cooked shrimp
> 1 tsp. celery salt
> ½ cup butter
> 1 tsp. salt
> ⅛ tsp. pepper
> dash of cayenne pepper

Grind shrimp or pound them into a paste in a mortar. Add butter and seasonings, mixing thoroughly. Place this paste in a small pan and bake at 350 degrees until mixture pulls away from sides of pan. Cool, then refrigerate. Slice for use on crackers or toast as an appetizer. Serves 3-4.

Pickled Shrimp

> 4 lbs. washed, peeled shrimp
> 1 tsp. dried red peppers
> ½ tsp. allspice
> 1 tsp. dill seed
> ½ tsp. dry mustard
> 2 tsp. fresh parsley, chopped
> 1 tsp. paprika
> 2 cups white vinegar
> 1 large onion, thinly sliced
> 2 limes, thinly sliced

Simmer seasonings in vinegar for about 30 minutes, then add shrimp and bring to a boiling point. Cook for about 5 minutes. Remove from heat and allow to cool. Add parsley. Place lime and onion slices over top. Add more liquid if necessary (⅓ cup of white vinegar, ⅔ cup of water, and 1 tsp. sugar). Serve shrimp chilled. Serves 3-4.

west Indian curried Shrimp

  2 lbs. peeled, deveined shrimp
  1 clove garlic, finely diced or crushed
  1 medium onion, sliced
  2 tbsp. lime juice
  2 tsp. curry powder
  1 cup of water or 1 cup coconut milk
  ¼ cup butter
  1 green mango (if available)

Fry onion and garlic lightly in butter. Add curry powder and chopped green mango, cooking for about 5 minutes. Add water or coconut milk obtained by adding hot water to equal amount of chopped or grated coconut meat and straining off liquid. Also add lime juice, salt, and pepper. Cook until mixture begins to thicken. Add shrimp and continue cooking until shrimp are tender. Serves 3-4.

In West Indies, a favorite companion to curried shrimp is fried bananas or plantains.

Shrimp Pilau

  1 lb. cooked shrimp
  ¼ cup chopped onions
  1 ½ cups uncooked rice
  ⅛ tsp. thyme
  3 cups cooked tomatoes
  3 slices of bacon, diced
  1 cup green pepper, diced

Fry bacon until crisp. Remove bacon. Saute onion and pepper in bacon fat. Add rice and tomatoes, cover and heat to boiling. Simmer for about 30 minutes. Reduce heat to low and allow to stand for about 15 minutes. Add shrimp and crisp bacon. Mix all ingredients and place in casserole dish. Bake at 350 degrees for 10-15 minutes. Serves 3-4.

Shrimp Pie

1 lb. cooked shrimp
1 chicken bouillon cube
1 can condensed mushroom soup
¼ cup green pepper, chopped
1 tsp. finely chopped parsley
1 tsp. salt
¾ cup celery, chopped
1 cup cooked corn
1 small onion, chopped
¼ cup butter, melted
⅛ tsp. cayenne pepper
¼ tsp. pepper

Cut shrimp into thirds or halves, depending on size. Dissolve bouillon cube in 1 cup of boiling water. Add mushroom soup and stir until smooth. Saute celery, onions, and green pepper. Add to the mushroom soup–chicken broth mixture and simmer for about 10 minutes. Add corn and shrimp, mixing thoroughly. Place mixture in a greased baking dish and cover top with a pie dough pastry folded over the edges of the baking dish and pricked with a fork in several places. Bake at 375 degrees for about 20 minutes. Serves 3-4.

Paella

Paella is a chicken and seafood mixture that could fit almost anywhere in the seafood section of this book and which also can be prepared in a variety of ways. The method suggested here is basic and fairly standard.

1 chicken, frying size cut into small pieces
2 chicken bouillon cubes
½ cup olive oil
1 tsp. paprika
1 medium-sized onion, chopped
1 ½ cups uncooked rice
2 tomatoes, cut in thick slices or wedges

½ tsp. pepper
1 lb. shrimp, peeled and deveined
1 pt. small clams, washed but in shells
1 cup lean pork cubes
2 cloves garlic, crushed
¼ tsp. saffron
1 tbsp. parsley, finely chopped
1 cup green pepper, chopped
2 tsp. salt
dash of cayenne pepper

Pour oil into large skillet or paella pan and cook chicken and pork until browned. Sprinkle with paprika. Add onion and cook for about 5 more minutes. Add crushed garlic and saffron, plus 2 tbsp. of chicken broth prepared from cubes. Place rice in pan and stir to coat with oil. Pour in remaining broth, stirring as added. Add salt and parsley, bringing mixture to boil and then simmering until rice is tender. Stir several times during the cooking process. Add all the remaining ingredients plus the shrimp and clams. Continue cooking until shrimp are done and clam shells are open. This will require about 10 minutes. Add more chicken broth if the paella begins to get too dry. In the West Indies, other items are added to paella almost at the whim of the cook. Squid and octopus are common additions. Serves 4-6.

SPINY LOBSTERS

Spiny lobsters, also called crawfish or Florida lobster, differ from the lobsters of northern waters in lacking large claws or pincers. Their protection is the numerous spines over their legs and body. Which is the more flavorful can stir heated disputes between native Floridians and northern visitors. Both are good, similar but distinctive.

In season, Florida spiny lobsters are available in many markets, most commonly already boiled and then refrigerated. If you get a live lobster, immerse it head first into salted, boiling water. Allow the water to return to boiling and to continue until lobster turns red. Split the lobster by placing it on its back and then cutting it

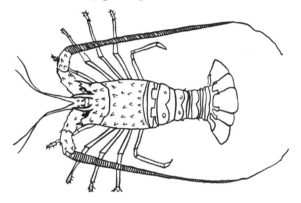

in half with a sharp knife. Most of the meat is in the tail, but some can be obtained also from the larger segments of the legs.

Lobster Salad

Cooked lobster cut into bite-sized pieces makes an excellent addition to a tossed salad, which then becomes a full meal. Diced lobster can be mixed with chopped pecans and chopped hard-boiled eggs combined with mayonnaise or French dressing. Serve on a lettuce leaf with wedges of tomato as a bordering garnish.

Broiled Lobster

2 lobsters, boiled and split
¼ tsp. salt
⅛ tsp. pepper
1 tbsp. melted butter
⅛ tsp. paprika
Tabasco sauce

Brush exposed meat with butter and sprinkle with salt, pepper and paprika. Add 2-3 drops of Tabasco to each if desired. Put lobsters about 4 inches from heat in broiler and cook until meat turns a very light brown. Generally served with a sauce made by combining ¼ cup melted butter with 1 tbsp. of lime juice. Season butter with garlic if desired. Serves 3-4.

Stuffed Crawfish

2 lobsters, split
2 medium-sized onions, chopped
1 tbsp. chopped parsley
¼ cup melted butter
1 tsp. Worcestershire sauce
4 stalks of celery, chopped
1 green pepper, diced
½ tsp. pepper
1 cup bread crumbs or croutons
⅛ tsp. dry mustard

Remove lobsters from shells, which are then thoroughly washed. Dice lobster meat. Saute in butter the onions, garlic, parsley, and celery, adding salt, pepper, dry mustard, and Worcestershire sauce. When onions have become light golden brown or glazed, add lobster meat and the bread crumbs or croutons. Mix thoroughly. Stuff the cleaned lobster shells with this mixture and bake for about 20 minutes at 400 degrees. Serves 2-4.

Bahamian Deviled Lobster

2 lobsters, boiled
2 tbsp. chopped peanuts
1 bay leaf
1 clove garlic, crushed
1 tbsp. sherry wine
2 tbsp. bread crumbs or croutons
2 tbsp. butter
1 tomato, chopped
1 small onion, chopped
1 lime
1 tsp. Worcestershire sauce

Remove lobsters from shells, which are then washed thoroughly and set aside. Dice lobster meat. In melted butter, cook gently for 10 minutes the tomatoes, peanuts, onion, garlic, bay leaf, sherry wine, Worcestershire sauce, lime juice, and bread crumbs. Add lobster meat and mix thoroughly, continuing cooking for an additional 5 minutes. Stuff the cleaned shells with this mixture. Sprinkle with grated cheddar or Parmesan cheese and brown in broiler before serving. Serves 3-4.

caribbean curried Lobster

2 lobsters, boiled and split
¼ cup melted butter
1 tbsp. grated fresh coconut
1 tbsp. curry powder
1 tsp. salt
2 tbsp. tomato paste
1 chicken bouillon cube
2 tbsp. olive oil
1 medium-sized onion, diced
1 green pepper, diced
2 tbsp. cooking sherry
⅛ tsp. pepper
½ tsp. turmeric

Use only the meat of the lobsters, frying in butter and oil until brown. Add onion, green pepper, grated coconut, and wine. Cook for an additional 5 minutes. Place in casserole, adding curry powder, turmeric, and tomato paste. Dissolve bouillon cube in ½ cup of hot water and add to contents of casserole. Liquid should cover contents of casserole. If not, add water. Season with salt and pepper. Bake for about 25 minutes at 375 degrees. If liquid is not thick at the end of this cooking time, add a white sauce made by combining ¼ cup milk, 1 tbsp. flour, and 1 tbsp. butter which is heated and stirred to make a smooth paste. Curried lobster is typically served on a bed of cooked rice. Serves 3-4.

Lobster with Almonds

1 or 2 lobsters, boiled and split
½ cup melted butter
¼ tsp. thyme
1 tbsp. chopped parsley
1 ½ cups blanched almonds
1 tsp. salt
⅛ tsp. pepper

Use only the tail meat, which is cut into bite-sized pieces. Saute almonds in butter until lightly browned. Remove almonds from frying pan and add lobster meat. Cook until browned. Add almonds and seasonings. Mix and heat thoroughly. Serves 3-4.

West Indian Lobster Fritters

2 lobsters, boiled and split
½ pint milk
1 tsp. pepper
⅛ tsp. cayenne
4 tbsp. flour
2 eggs plus 3 hardcooked egg yolks
¼ tsp. pepper

Chop or grind lobster meat, mixing in egg yolks, cayenne, salt, and pepper. Break raw eggs into sifted flour and beat, adding milk and continuing to beat until batter is formed. Add lobster meat. Form spoon-sized balls of lobsters and batter. Fry in butter until browned on all sides. Serves 3-4.

Lobster and Rice Surprise

2 lobsters, meat removed and diced
2 bay leaves
¼ lb. butter
1 small (4 oz.) can mushrooms
1 small can pimentos

1 small can anchovies
2 medium-sized onions, diced
2 cloves garlic, crushed
⅛ tsp. saffron
¼ cup sherry
1 ½ cups rice
1 chicken bouillon cube
grated cheddar cheese or Parmesan

Saute onions and garlic in butter. Add lobster meat, rice, pimentos, and anchovies, plus the bay leaves, saffron, salt, and pepper. Dissolve bouillon cube in ¼ cup hot water, add sherry, and pour over the lobster and seasonings. Bring to a boil and simmer for about 10 minutes. Transfer to a greased baking dish and bake for about 20 minutes at 400 degrees. Sprinkle with grated cheese and return to oven only long enough for cheese to melt. Serves 4-6.

Lobster Thermidor

2 lobsters, boiled and split
½ cup cooked mushrooms
2 cups cream
1 egg yolk
1 tsp. salt
Tabasco sauce
¼ cup melted butter
½ tsp. paprika
¼ cup sherry wine
⅛ tsp. thyme
¼ tsp. pepper

Remove meat from shells, which are then washed thoroughly and set aside. Dice lobster meat and saute with mushrooms in melted butter. Sprinkle lobster with paprika, add thyme, and cook on medium heat for 2-3 minutes. Keep stirred. Blend egg yolk with cream and pour over the seasoned lobster. Add salt, pepper, and 2-3 drops of Tabasco. Cook for 3-5 minutes. Fill lobster shells with this mixture. Cover with grated cheddar cheese and place under broiler. Remove as soon as cheese melts and begins to brown. Serves 2-4.

CRABS

Two kinds of edible crabs are harvested from Florida waters: the blue crab, which is called soft-shell crab when it is taken after its old shell has been shed and before the new one hardens; and the stone crab, which many rate as the aristocrat of the shellfish. Only the huge claw of the stone crab is eaten, the crab itself returned to the water where it grows a new replacement claw. They are harvested from late fall through spring, allowing them the full summer to propagate.

Blue crabs are found in many bays and estuaries. Sometimes they migrate across land in large numbers and may be found miles from water. The live crabs are cooked in boiling, salted water for 20-30 minutes or until the crab becomes orange. Drain and wash the cooked crabs several times and then allow to cool. Remove the claws and legs, cracking and extracting meat from large segments. Pull the top shell away gently, wash and save for use in baking. Lift out the digestive tract and then wash insides. Split tail section and remove meat, using a nut pick where necessary.

Soft-shell crabs are prepared for cooking by inserting point of knife between the eyes, then lifting off the back shell by grasping the pointed ends of the shell. The gills and sand bag will pull away with the shell. Turn the crab over and, using knife to help, lift off the central body plate (apron). Wash the crabs thoroughly and then cook immediately.

Deviled Crabs

 2 cups chopped crab meat
 1 small onion, finely diced
 1 cup chicken bouillon
 1 tsp. prepared mustard

¼ tsp. pepper
Tabasco sauce
1 cup cracker crumbs (or bread)
¼ cup melted butter
2 eggs, lightly beaten
½ tsp. salt
⅛ tsp. thyme
Parmesan

Mix crab meat, egg, bouillon, butter, and all seasonings (2-3 drops of Tabasco) with ½ cup of cracker crumbs. Place this mixture in washed crab shells. Top with remaining crumbs and sprinkle with Parmesan cheese. Bake at 375 degrees until crumbs have turned toasty brown. Serves 3-4.

Like lobsters and shrimp, cold, cooked crab meat makes an excellent addition to almost any lettuce-based salad and accepts both vinegar and oil or creamy-type dressings.

Crab Soup

1 cup cooked crab meat
2 eggs
2 tbsp. vinegar
1 tsp. salt
¼ tsp. pepper
1 qt. chicken broth
2 tomatoes, chopped
2 tbsp. olive oil
1 small onion, finely chopped
⅛ tsp. paprika

Saute crab meat in oil with tomatoes. In the West Indies, ½ tsp. of freshly grated ginger root is also added. Pour chicken broth over crab meat and simmer for about 10 minutes. Beat eggs and mix with onions, vinegar, salt, pepper, and paprika. Add to simmering soup and continue cooking at low heat until seasonings are thoroughly blended. Serve hot. Serves 3-4.

Fried Soft-shell Crabs

Put freshly cleaned crabs in salt solution consisting of 2 tsp. of salt and 1 tsp. of lime juice for each cup of water. Allow to stand for 5–10 minutes. Drain crabs and dip them first into beaten eggs and then into cracker crumbs or bread crumbs. Cook in deep fat heated to 360 degrees until they turn golden brown. If they rise to top of oil, turn them to make certain they cook on all sides. Drain on absorbent paper towel. Usually eaten with tartar sauce.

Caribbean Crab Croquettes

> 3 cups crab meat
> 1 onion, diced
> 1 tsp. salt
> 2 eggs, beaten
> 1 cup cracker crumbs
> ¼ tsp. thyme or mace
> ¼ tsp. pepper
> 1 tsp. Worcestershire sauce

Mix finely chopped or ground crab meat with seasonings and blend in a cup of thick white sauce made by combining 4 tbsp. flour, 4 tbsp. butter, 1 tsp. salt, and a dash of pepper with 1 cup of milk. Cook on medium heat until thickens. Allow mixture to chill, then form croquettes that are rolled first in cracker crumbs and then in eggs. Give them a final coating of cracker crumbs. Cook in deep fat at 400 degrees, removing when browned. Serves 3–4.

Spicy Crab Casserole

> 1 cup cooked crab meat
> 2 cups macaroni
> 1 can (4 oz.) mushrooms
> 1 medium-sized onion, sliced
> 1 clove garlic, crushed
> ⅛ tsp. pepper
> ⅛ tsp. cayenne

1 tbsp. lime juice
1 cup grated cheddar cheese
½ cup sour cream
2 tomatoes, sliced
1 cup celery, chopped
1 tsp. salt

Cut crab meat into small pieces and sprinkle with lime juice. Cook macaroni and drain. Add sour cream, mushrooms, and seasoning to macaroni and mix gently to spread the cream and seasonings throughout. Put macaroni on bottom of a greased baking dish. Spread over it a layer of the tomato and onion slices. Next add a layer of crab meat, using all. Top with remaining onions and tomatoes and season them with salt and pepper. Spread grated cheddar over the top and bake in oven at 375 degrees for about 20 minutes. Serves 4.

FRESHWATER CATFISH

Milk-Marinated Bullheads à la Veda

6-8 bullheads, 1½-1¾ lb. each
milk
3 tbsp. butter
flour
⅛-¼ tsp. pepper
salt
lime juice
cooking oil

Soak cleaned catfish in salted water for at least 15 minutes. Remove from water and place in bowl. Cover completely with milk, adding 1 tbsp. of salt and ⅛-¼ tsp. pepper. Marinate in milk for 6 hours or longer. Drain, then sprinkle with salt, pepper, and flour. Fry in deep fat until crisp. Turn heat down and allow to simmer for about half an hour. Drain. Put fish in skillet with 3 tbsp. of butter. Sprinkle with lime juice and cook for 10-15 minutes on medium heat. The result is crisped catfish with an unsurpassable flavor.

While the oil is hot, make some hushpuppies, the perfect companions for catfish.

Hushpuppies

2 cups cornmeal
1 tbsp. flour
½ tsp. baking soda
1 tsp. salt
1 egg, beaten
3 tbsp. onion, finely diced
1 cup buttermilk

Mix all the dry ingredients, then add the egg, onion, and buttermilk. Stir thoroughly. Drop by about ½ tbsp. at a time into hot, deep fat. Remove as soon as they float. The above should produce about 1 ½ dozen.

Note: Variations in making hushpuppies are numerous in the South where they are traditional favorites. The above is a good basic recipe. Onions may be omitted if preferred.

3.

Vegetables

SWEET CORN

Florida winter visitors are generally delighted to find sweet corn and other vegetables in season in the southern half of the state when most of the country is having freezing weather. Sweet corn can be bought at vegetable markets or picked in the fields by following the guiding arrows of U-Pick signs. The corn is used, of course, in the same ways as anywhere, eaten either on the cob or cut off for addition to various dishes of the cook's choice. A few Florida variations are suggested here.

Avocado Spread for Corn

> 1 avocado, mashed
> 1 clove garlic, crushed
> 2 tsp. lime juice
> 1 tsp. salt
> ⅛ tsp. pepper
> Tabasco sauce

Combine the above ingredients, mixing thoroughly. Use instead of butter when eating corn-on-the-cob, whether grilled or steamed.

Florida Corn and Shrimp

> 3 cups fresh corn, cut from cob
> 1 ½ cups cooked shrimp

1 tbsp. lime juice
1 medium-sized onion, diced
¼ cup butter, melted
¼ tsp. sugar
1 tsp. salt
⅛ tsp. pepper

Saute corn in butter, adding sugar. Cook until corn is tender, then add onions, lime juice, salt and pepper. Cook for about 5 minutes additional on moderate heat. Add cooked shrimp to heat. Serves 3-4.

Corn and Squash

2 cups fresh corn, cut from cob
2 tomatoes, diced
1 lb. yellow squash, sliced
1 medium onion, diced
2 tbsp. olive oil
2 tsp. salt
½ tsp. sugar
¼ tsp. pepper
½ tsp. oregano

Saute onions in oil, then add corn, squash, tomatoes, and seasonings. Continue cooking at moderate heat for about 20 minutes or until corn is tender. Serves 4-6.

Note: Also good with zucchini squash or a combination of the two.

Deep-fat Corn Fritters

3 cups of corn, cut from cob
1 tsp. salt
2 tbsp. melted butter
½ cup milk
1 cup flour
1 egg, beaten
1 tsp. baking powder

⅛ *tsp. pepper*
cooking oil

Mix egg with milk and then stir in the flour, baking powder, salt, and pepper. Add the corn and melted butter. Mixture should be thick. If not, add more corn. Drop by the spoonful into cooking oil heated to 375 degrees and cook until browned on all sides. Serves 3-4.

Fried Corn

3 *cups corn, cut from cob*
1 *green pepper, chopped*
1 *medium-sized onion, chopped*
1 ½ *tsp. salt*
¼ *tsp. pepper*
4 *slices of bacon*

Fry bacon until crisp. Remove from skillet, drain, and crumble. Add corn, green pepper, and onion to bacon drippings in skillet. Cover and cook on low heat until vegetables are just tender. This will require only 6-8 minutes. Season with salt and pepper, and sprinkle crumbled bacon over the top. Serves 4-6.

Corn and Oysters

2 *cups corn, cut from cob*
1 *pt. shucked oysters*
¼ *cup bread crumbs*
2 *tbsp. butter*
1 ½ *tsp. salt*
¼ *tsp. pepper*

Grease casserole dish. Put a layer of corn on bottom, then a layer of oysters, and finally a sprinkled layer of bread crumbs. Add salt and pepper. Repeat. In an average casserole dish, the above ingredients will make about 3 layers. Dot the top layer of bread crumbs with butter. Bake at 350 degrees for 25–30 minutes. Serves 3-4.

Note: The above is equally good with scallops. For a variation, add 2–3 tomatoes, cut either in slices or in wedges. If neither oysters nor scallops can be had, the casserole is good with only the addition of tomatoes or with a small amount (about ¼ cup) of chopped ham.

MALANGAS

Malangas are now grown on many hundreds of acres in the farm lands south of Miami. Newcomers are likely to think these are "elephant ear" ornamentals being grown for sale as potted plants. True, the plants are related and look much alike, but the ornamentals are not edible (many plants in this group contain a poisonous juice). Malangas, in contrast, are one of the favorite starchy foods of the Caribbean, particularly in Cuba. It is the Cuban colony in the Miami area that makes up most of the malanga market, naturally, but a growing number of Florida newcomers from the north and longtime residents are also learning to appreciate the distinctive but potato-like qualities of the malanga.

Malanga plants produce thick underground stems on which mature plants also bear roundish, potato-sized outgrowths. It is these underground portions that are cooked. First the tough outer stem is peeled off to reveal the white-fleshed inner portion. The stem is cut into cooking-sized pieces (an inch or two long, or potato-sized), and boiled in salted water until tender. In cooking older stems in particular, the water should be drained and replaced with new water at least twice.

Malangas can be utilized in all of the ways white potatoes are cooked. The almost slippery texture of the cooked malanga may at first be objectionable because it is natural to compare the vegetable to the more familiar and mealy white potato. But when the malanga is eaten simply because it is good in its own way and without making a comparison (the greatest similarity is that both are starchy foods), the malanga stands out as delightful.

Those who live in southern Florida may want to grow their own malangas. The plants are attractive and can contribute to landscaping while at the same time providing food whenever it is needed. Further, the young leaves, clipped as they are just beginning to unfold, can be cooked like spinach or other greens.

Malanga Fritters

1 ½ lbs. of malangas, cut into small pieces for cooking
1 egg
1 small onion, diced
¼ tsp. baking powder
1 ½ tbsp. flour
1 tsp. salt
¼ tsp. pepper
cooking oil

Cook malangas in lightly salted water until tender. Drain and put them in a bowl. Mash with a spoon or a potato masher, while at the same time mixing in the flour, onion, egg, salt, pepper, and baking powder. Heat cooking oil in deep-fat fryer to 375 degrees. Drop malanga mixture into heated oil a spoonful at a time. Remove when browned and place on paper towels to drain. These fritters are generally eaten immediately, but they are also good when cold. Serves 3-4.

YAMS

Yams of the subtropics are not the same as sweet potatoes, which are sometimes called yams in the United States. The true yam belongs to an entirely different family of plants, which is represented in the subtropics by several hundred species of vines and shrubs.

Yams are underground stems or tubers of vines. In some species, the flesh of the yam is white; in others, yellowish. Many yams weigh a pound each. The giant of the clan is a Latin American yam that may be as much as six feet long and weigh a hundred pounds.

Like malangas, yams can be utilized in the same way as the familiar white potatoes and sweet potatoes. On many islands in the West Indies, for example, yam chips are as popular as potato chips are in temperate regions. Yams also make excellent fritters, prepared in the same way as malanga fritters.

West Indian Scalloped Yams

1 ½ lbs. yams, sliced
1 large onion, sliced
¼ lb. butter
3 cups coconut milk (or regular milk)
1 ½ tsp. salt
¼ tsp. pepper
½ cup grated cheese

Obtain coconut milk by pouring hot water over freshly grated coconut meat and then pressing the coconut to get out the fluid. Strain, saving the liquid. Precook yams in lightly salted water until slices begin to be tender. Grease casserole dish with butter, then add the yams and onions in layers, salting and peppering each layer. Add the coconut milk (or regular homogenized milk). Cook in oven at 350 degrees until yams are completely tender and top of casserole begins to brown. Remove from oven and dot top with butter, spreading grated cheese over the top. Return to oven only long enough for the cheese to melt. Serves 3-4.

Yam Cakes

2 lbs. yams
2 eggs, lightly beaten
¼ cup bread crumbs
3 tsp. butter
1 tsp. salt
¼ tsp. pepper

Boil yams in lightly salted water until tender. Drain and mash, mixing the salt and pepper, eggs, and bread crumbs. Form into patties and fry in butter until browned on one side, then turn and brown the other. Serves 3-4.

For a variation, add cheese or diced onions (or both) to the mixture before frying.

BANANAS

In temperate regions, bananas are thought of only for eating raw or in making various desserts. Their uses in this manner are treated in the dessert section of this book. Here the banana is considered only as a vegetable. The most common of the bananas used in this way is the plantain, which can be grown throughout southern Florida. The plants add handsomely to a tropical landscaping. Plantains can also be bought in many markets. They are used most commonly when mature but still green, just beginning to turn in color. At this stage they consist mainly of starch, which does not change to sugar until the fruit ripens. The simplest way to prepare them is by boiling, whole or sliced, in lightly salted water and serving with butter, salt and pepper.

Jamaican Fried Plantains

4-5 plantains
¼ cup flour
1 tsp. cinnamon
¼ cup butter

Peel plantains and then either slice them crosswise or lengthwise. Wash the pieces in cold water; dry thoroughly. Sprinkle with flour and cinnamon and then fry in butter until golden brown. Serves 3-4.

Florida Fried Plantains

4-5 plantains, peeled and sliced
2 tbsp. cooking oil (olive, peanut, butter, or other)
1 tsp. salt
¼ tsp. pepper
1 clove garlic, crushed

Heat oil and add garlic, cooking until it turns brown. Add plantain slices and fry until they turn golden. Sprinkle with salt and pepper. Serves 3-4.

Plantain Chips

4-5 plantains, peeled and sliced very thin
salt
cooking oil

Make certain plantains are cut very thin, like potato chips. Fry them in oil until they are a crisp brown. Drain on paper towels and add salt. In the islands, these are referred to as mariquitos, and they can be bought already packaged in markets. They are available this way also in Florida. Serves 3-4.

Bananas and Ham

2 firm plantains or bananas, peeled and sliced
2 slices of ham, each about an inch thick
¼ cup brown sugar
4 tbsp. grated coconut
4 tbsp. lime juice
¼ stick of butter

Cut ham slices in half and put in a shallow, greased baking dish. Cover with banana slices. Sprinkle with lime juice and sugar. Spread coconut over the top and then dot with butter. Bake for about 30 minutes in oven preheated to 350 degrees. Serves 4.

Green Plantains, Boiled

2-3 plantains, green and unspotted

3 slices of bacon

1 medium onion, chopped

1 small green pepper, chopped

1 lime, cut into wedges

butter

salt

pepper

Peel plantains and cut into pieces about 2 inches long. (Peeling is best done under cold running water.) Immediately put them in a saucepan of salted, boiling water. Cover. Cook until soft. Drain and put on absorbent paper towels. Fry bacon until crisp, then put on paper towels. Pour off most of bacon drippings in skillet, then fry onion and green pepper until soft and just turning brown. Cut plantains into smaller pieces and mix with the onions, pepper, and bacon (crumbled). Add butter, salt and pepper to taste. Garnish with lime wedges and serve while hot. Serves 4-6.

BREADFRUIT

Brought to the West Indies from the Pacific by Captain Bligh of the Bounty, the breadfruit is now a staple on many of the islands. It is available in limited quantities in specialty markets of extreme southern Florida. The plants are grown also as novelty ornamentals, and an increasing number of people are appreciating the fruit that their plants produce. Breadfruit trees may grow to as much as 50 feet tall.

The round, seedless fruit typically weigh two or three pounds, occasionally as much as ten. Their name comes from the breadlike flavor and texture of the immature fruit. Breadfruit can be fried (then it tastes most like potatoes), steamed, baked, or boiled. Thin slices are deep-fat fried like plantains or potatoes to make bread-fruit chips.

Cold Breadfruit Salad

1 breadfruit, boiled and diced
3 stalks of celery, diced as fine or finer than breadfruit
1 large onion, chopped
vinegar
oil
salt
pepper

Combine breadfruit, celery, and onion. Stir in a mixture of oil and vinegar (2 parts oil, 1 part vinegar) until thoroughly moist. Season to taste with salt and pepper. Chill before serving. Serves 3-4.

Stuffed Breadfruit

2 breadfruit
½ lb. hamburger
¼ lb. sausage
1 tomato, chopped
1 medium-sized onion, chopped
salt and pepper

Parboil peeled breadfruit whole in salted water. Fry hamburger and sausage until browned. Pour off excess grease from sausage, then stir in the tomato and onion, seasoning the mixture to taste with salt and pepper. Cut out the cores of the now cooled breadfruit and take out also enough flesh to accommodate the stuffing mixture. Pack both breadfruits with stuffing and then bake for about 45 minutes, or until soft and brown, in oven preheated to 350 degrees. Before serving, spread a little butter over the breadfruit. Serves 4.

AVOCADOS

Avocados are a fruit that can be eaten either as a vegetable, mainly in salads, or as a dessert. Originally native to the American subtropical lowlands, the avocado has been spread to warm climates throughout the world. In southern Florida, many are grown as dooryard ornamentals. South of Miami, they are also produced commercially in groves. By shopping roadside stands or buying directly from the growers, those with a well-developed taste for this fruit can often get their fill at bargain prices.

Most consumers simply buy "an avocado," but there are actually dozens of varieties. Some weigh three pounds or more; others are no larger than oranges. Some ooze oil when cut; others are mealy or crumbly. Some have light yellowish-green skins; others are dark purplish, commonly tinged with scarlet. They vary in shape from oval or egg-shaped to round like a grapefruit, pear-shaped, or long and slim, resembling large cucumbers or zucchini squash. The kind most commonly pictured is pear shaped. One common variety of this shape is particularly susceptible to infestation by scale insects that produce scaly patches on the skin of the fruit. These look much like alligator skin, which is probably what gave rise to the common name of "alligator pear" that is used generally for avocados in Florida.

Inside, the greenish to egg-yolk yellow flesh of the different varieties of avocados is equally varied in texture and flavor. Some are definitely buttery in consistency. Other kinds have a distinctly nutty flavor. The great advantage of avocados aside from their own good flavor is that they are bland enough to accept all types of seasonings and mix well with nearly all other vegetables. Avocados are generally eaten raw. They may be added to soups or as a final addition to other cooked dishes, but they do not withstand cooking well themselves.

An avocado is ripe and ready to be eaten when it begins to soften or is pliable. Hold the avocado between your hands and press gently but firmly. If you feel the fruit "give" to the pressure, it is ready to be eaten. If it is still firm, wait another day or two. If you are in a hurry, put the avocado in a warm place and keep it out of the direct sun. You can speed up the ripening by putting the avocado in a brown paper bag and closing the top. If you have two avocados, put them both in the bag; the ripening process will be greatly accelerated. To retard ripening, put avocados in refrigerator.

After an avocado is cut, the flesh will darken quickly if it is not used in a short time. If you are using only half the avocado, leave the seed in the saved half. This retards the darkening. Also rub the exposed portions with lime juice. If you are making dips or using the avocado in other ways that necessitate letting it stand for a while, make certain lime juice is spread over the exposed avocado or into the mixture to act as a buffer against the blackening process.

The recipes here are for the use of the avocado as a vegetable. Dessert recipes are given elsewhere in the book.

Avocado Dip (Guacamole)

1 avocado (2 if small; 3-4 if California avocados)
1 medium-sized onion, diced
Tabasco (optional)
1 tbsp. lime juice
½ tsp. chili powder (optional)
1 clove garlic, crushed
salt and pepper to taste

Peel avocado, remove seed, and mash in a bowl, using fork or a potato masher. Add lime juice, onion, garlic, and seasonings, stirring them in thoroughly. Add salt and pepper to taste, plus 2-3 drops of Tabasco if you want to pep up the dip. By varying the amount of lime juice only slightly, you will also make the dip thicker or thinner, for use either as a spread or with thin chips. For interesting canapes, cut slices of cucumber diagonally and spread with guacamole.

Variations in making guacamole are almost limitless. As a few examples, use ⅔ mashed avocado and ⅓ cottage cheese. For different seasonings, try a dash or two of curry powder. Bits of crisp bacon added to the avocado make an interesting variation; some people prefer finely chopped chicken or turkey. For still another, add about 2 tbsp. of finely chopped nuts (peanuts, cashews, or mixed). Instead of lime juice, use ½ tbsp. of mayonnaise and 1 tsp. of Worcestershire sauce. Finely chopped celery, green pepper, tomatoes, olives—all are good and help make avocado dips distinctive and exciting.

Avocado Halves

½ avocado for each serving
salt
pepper
lime juice
garlic powder (or crushed cloves)

Cut avocado in half and remove seed. Sprinkle surface of avocado with salt, pepper, and garlic powder (the latter is optional). Mix ⅓ olive oil with ⅔ lime juice and coat exposed surface of avocado. Serve ½ avocado to each person. Note: This is the very basic method of preparation. Variations are many. French dressing can be used in place of the olive oil and lime juice. Vinegar can be substituted for the lime juice. Some prefer mayonnaise. The seasonings can also be varied in their kind and amount. Start with the basic preparation described above and work from it to arrive at variations that you find most satisfying. Some kinds of avocados demand more seasonings than others, whereas a mealy, nutty-flavored avocado needs almost no seasoning.

Stuffed Avocado

Cut avocado in half and remove seed, preparing ½ avocado per serving. Sprinkle exposed surface with lime juice, salt, and pepper. Fill the seed cavity—and you can mound it—with one of the following, or you can improvise (avocados inspire one to do so).

1. cooked lobster, shrimp, or crabmeat mixed with tomatoes, chopped olives, celery, onions, and green pepper. Season to taste with salt and pepper.

2. chopped ham, turkey, or chicken, mixed with diced, celery, green pepper, pimento, and mayonnaise. Season mixture to taste with salt and pepper.

Avocados in Salads

Because the avocado is so adaptable, it makes an excellent addition to almost any fruit or vegetable salad, from the simplest lettuce and avocado combination to a complex tossed salad of many components. The avocado can be cut into wedges and used as a garnish around the edge of the salad dish or bowl, or it can be cut into smaller pieces and mixed throughout the salad.

To spread an avocado flavor through a salad, even if chunks of avocado are omitted, put 1 tbsp. of lime juice in the bottom of the salad bowl before adding other vegetables. Sprinkle a bit of garlic powder into the juice or crush a clove of garlic and add about ¼ tsp. of salt (the garlic and salt are optional). Add 1-2 small slices of avocado to the lime juice and mash with a fork, mixing the avocado thoroughly with the lime juice. Build the salad above this mixture. When the salad is tossed, the lime juice and avocado will be spread throughout. Additional salad dressing of your choice must be added to the salad, of course.

CABBAGE

Cultivated for more than 4,000 years, the many varieties of cabbage are grown in both temperate and subtropical regions, both commercially and by home gardeners. They favor cool regions. Again, travelers or new residents in the warm parts of Florida and in the islands will find fresh cabbage on the market in stores and at roadside stands at times of the year when it cannot be grown in temperate climates. Most people will use cabbage in the ways familiar to them-steamed, boiled, in cole slaw, or as an addition to soups or stews. For the best flavor, cook cabbage briefly. It should still be crisp, still retaining its vitamins. Do not cook until the cabbage is nothing more than a soggy tasteless mass. Here are a few variations, à la Florida and the subtropics:

Cabbage Soup with Shrimp

1 head of cabbage, shredded
1 cup of shrimp, peeled and deveined
1 medium-sized onion, diced
1 qt. water
2 tbsp. butter or 1 tbsp. olive oil
1 ½ tsp. salt
¼ tsp. pepper
¼ tsp. caraway seed

Saute shrimp in butter or olive oil in deep saucepan. Add water, cabbage, onions, and seasonings. Cook on low heat until cabbage is just tender. Do not overcook. Serves 4-6.

Variations include addition of different seasonings, such as several drops of Tabasco sauce, ½ tsp. freshly ground ginger (or ginger powder as a substitute), 1 tsp. of parsley. Among the vegetables that can be included are diced malangas or potatoes, carrots, chayotes, celery, and green peppers, which heads a simple cabbage and shrimp soup quickly in the direction of becoming a full-fledged fresh vegetable soup. This is perfectly all right, too.

Florida Smothered Cabbage

1 medium-sized head of cabbage
3 slices of bacon, diced
1 tsp. salt
¼ tsp. pepper

Fry bacon until crisp. Remove from skillet and place on absorbent towel. Shred cabbage and add to skillet with salt and pepper. Cover and cook on low heat for about 20 minutes. Sprinkle with crisp bacon pieces and serve. This is excellent with a good hot pepper-sauce made of hot peppers in vinegar. Serves 3-4.

Caribbean Cabbage with Capers

1 medium to large head of cabbage, shredded
2 tbsp. capers
2 slices bacon, diced
¼ tsp. pepper
2 tomatoes, diced
1 cup cooked ham, chopped
1 medium-sized onion, diced
2 tbsp. vinegar
1 clove garlic, crushed
1 tsp. salt
½ cup croutons

Fry bacon until crisp, remove from frying pan and drain on absorbent paper towel. Saute onions and garlic in bacon fat. Add shredded cabbage, tomatoes, capers, vinegar, salt, pepper, and about ½ cup of water. Mix thoroughly and continue cooking on medium heat until cabbage is tender. Add the cooked ham. Sprinkle with croutons and crisp bacon before serving. Serves 4-6.

West Indian Slaw

1 medium head of cabbage, shredded
2 apples, chopped
6 slices pineapple, fresh if possible
2 tbsp. green pepper, chopped
4 tbsp. grated carrots
1 tsp. salt
1 tsp. sugar
2 tbsp. vinegar

Combine cabbage, apples and green pepper. Mix salt, sugar, and vinegar, stirring until salt and sugar are dissolved. Pour over the cabbage mixture. Sprinkle grated carrots over the mixture, then put pineapple slices on top. Use immediately. Serves 4-6.

COLLARDS

Collards, like kale, are a headless kind of cabbage. They are unfamiliar to most northerners but have long been popular in the Deep South of which North Florida is a part. Collard greens appear regularly in vegetable markets in Florida in winter, their abundance increasing toward the Georgia border. The recipes here are simply to acquaint newcomers with this cabbage-flavored green.

Steamed Collards

1 lb. collard greens
1 tsp. salt
¼ tsp. pepper
1 slice bacon
⅛ lb. butter

Wash the greens, cutting away the thick midribs of the leaves. Steam or boil gently in lightly salted water until tender. Fry bacon until crisp, remove from frying pan and crumble. Sprinkle bacon bits over collards and season with salt and pepper, mixing thoroughly in serving bowl. Dot with butter. Serves 3-4.

For a variation, add grated cheese to top and put bowl in oven to melt cheese before serving.

Fried Collards

 1 lb. collard greens
 2 slices salt pork, diced
 1 tsp. salt
 ¼ tsp. pepper

Prepare collards as above, then chop finely. Add to salted, boiling water and cook briefly—only until collards begin to be tender. Remove and drain. Fry salt pork (or bacon) until brown. Add collards to frying pan and continue to cook, stirring constantly, until the collards are tender. Season with salt and pepper. As with cabbage, a vinegar-pepper sauce makes an excellent condiment. Serves 3-4.

RADISHES

Radishes grow so rapidly that many people like to grow their own in home gardens. In Florida, they are abundantly available in winter from commercial plantings. The two common kinds are small, round red radishes and the long icicle or white radishes. Those who grow their own experiment with some of the numerous other kinds, including the very large black radishes.

Radishes are most commonly eaten raw, either individually or as an addition to salads. Fewer people are aware that radishes can also be cooked like turnips, which they resemble in flavor but are more zesty. A few radishes sliced and added to rice and seafood casseroles during the cooking add a distinctive difference to the dish. Radishes can also be preserved in a briny vinegar, like pickles.

Radish Salad

> 2 packages red radishes
> 1 package white radishes
> 1 bunch green onions
> salt
> pepper
> homogenized milk

This salad is an unusual way of using radishes to make a perfect companion for steaks. Wash radishes and onions. Slice radishes as thin as possible (it is the easiest with a potato peeler), and cut onions crosswise into ¼ to ½ inch pieces, including much of the tops. Put both radishes and onions in a bowl and cover with water to which enough salt is added to make a strong briny solution. Allow to stand for at least 3 hours. Do not cover. Just before mealtime, pour off the water, pushing down on the contents to squeeze out all of the water possible. Loosen the compacted radishes and onions by stirring them a bit, then pour over them just enough cold homogenized milk to cover. Sprinkle liberally with pepper, coarse or freshly ground preferred. Stir contents thoroughly. Serves 3-4.

BEANS

The dozens of different kinds of beans are a staple in many subtropical regions. Most of the kinds described here are familiar, but the recipes have a Florida or subtropical flavor. Some are abundantly available fresh in Florida in winter, particularly green (string or snap) that are produced in large quantities for the northern vegetable markets.

Green Beans and Eggplant, Caribbean Style

> 1 lb. green beans, washed and snapped
> 1 eggplant, peeled and cubed

1 cucumber, peeled and diced
1 small can of bean sprouts
1 tomato, peeled and sliced
2 hardcooked eggs
1 tsp. salt
¼ tsp. pepper

In a saucepan, bring one cup of lightly salted water to boil. Add beans and bring to boil again. Reduce heat to medium and add bean sprouts, diced cucumber, and eggplant. Cook until tender, seasoning to taste with salt and pepper. Place beans in serving bowl and top with slices of tomato and hardcooked eggs before serving. Serves 4-6.

Bahamian Bean Soup

1 lb. green beans, cut French style
2 tomatoes, chopped
1 potato, diced
1 carrot, sliced
¼ cup shredded cabbage
1 onion, diced
1 stalk celery, chopped
2 tbsp. cooked rice
½ tsp. pepper
2 slices of bacon, diced
1/5 pound lean pork, cut in small pieces
1 clove garlic, crushed
1 bay leaf
¼ tsp. thyme
1 small can tomato paste
1 ½ tsp. salt

Cook bacon and pork in deep saucepan or kettle. Add all of the vegetables except the potato and continue cooking for about 5 minutes. Stir constantly. Reduce heat. Add 1 ½ qts. water, tomato paste, potato, rice, and all seasonings. Mix thoroughly and allow to simmer for about 2 hours. Serves 3-4.

KIDNEY BEANS

Bahamian Beans and Pork

1 lb. dry kidney beans
½ lb. salt pork
1 medium-sized onion, chopped
1 clove garlic, crushed
2 tbsp. Worcestershire sauce
2 tbsp. brown sugar
1 ½ tsp. salt
½ tsp. pepper
⅛ cup vinegar

Wash beans and then soak for a minimum of 3 hours, or overnight if possible. Add more water if necessary, covering beans. Bring water to a boil, then reduce heat and allow beans to cook slowly until they are tender. Cut pork in small pieces and place in baking dish large enough to hold the beans. Mix the onions, garlic, and seasonings with the beans and the liquid in which they are cooked. Place beans in baking dish and stir all contents. Bake for 2 hours at 375 degrees. Stir several times, adding water ¼ cup at a time to prevent beans from sticking. Serves 3-4.

RED PEAS (BEANS)

Red Pea Soup

Note: The red pea, or bean, is a favorite throughout the West Indies for a wide variety of rice and meat dishes.

1 lb. dry red beans
¼ lb. salt pork
1 medium-sized onion, chopped
2 qts. of water
Tabasco
salt

Wash peas, place them in water, and bring to a vigorous boil. Reduce heat. Add the diced salt pork, onion, and several drops of Tabasco, continuing to cook on low heat for 2-3 hours, or until the red peas are tender. Salt to taste and serve. Serves 4-6.

Note: The above soup can also be made with either pinto or Navy beans, but the red peas have a distinctive flavor and should be used if possible. In Florida, shop the markets catering to Latin Americans.

Red Peas with Rice and Ham

½ lb. dried red peas
¼ lb. cooked, diced ham
1 medium-sized onion, diced
⅛ tsp. thyme
¼ tsp. pepper
½ lb. rice
1 bay leaf
1 clove garlic, crushed
1 tsp. salt

Place washed red peas in saucepan, cover with water, and bring to a vigorous boil. Reduce heat, add tomatoes, onions, garlic, bay leaf, thyme, salt and pepper. Simmer until peas are tender. Cook rice in separate pan and drain. Add seasoned peas and ham to cooked rice and mix thoroughly. Adjust salt and pepper to taste. Reheat and serve. This dish, with many local variations, is a favorite throughout the Bahamas and West Indies and goes by a number of different names. Serves 3-4.

BLACK BEANS

Black beans are used throughout the American tropics. Their flavor is as distinctive as their appearance. Black beans and yellow rice is served regularly as a main course.

Black Beans and Yellow Rice

1 ½ cups black beans, or 2 standard size cans of precooked
1 package of yellow rice
1 large onion, diced

If you use canned beans, it's a simple matter of opening the cans and heating the beans. If you use dried beans, soak them overnight before cooking. Follow the directions on the package to give them seasoning while soaking. You can also add 1 clove of crushed garlic, 1 small onion diced, 1 stalk of chopped celery, 1 ½ tsp. prepared mustard, 1 tbsp. olive oil, 1 tsp. salt, and ½ tsp. black pepper. After soaking put beans and the water in which they soaked in a large enough pot and bring to a boil. Then lower heat and cook slowly until beans are tender. Add water as needed but keep the level low—just enough to keep the beans covered.

When beans are tender and ready to serve, cook the rice, again following the directions on the package. Serve in a flat soup bowl or a deep plate. Put rice in one half of the bowl or plate, then fill the other half with black beans. Add diced raw onion liberally down the middle. Eat with a spoon or a fork, picking up a combination of the rice, beans, and some onion. Serves 3-4.

Note: If you feel black beans and yellow rice are not quite enough, you can add two or three slices of boned chicken at the outer edge of the black beans and yellow rice. If you like seasonings, add 1 large onion chopped, 1 bay leaf, 1 ½ tsp. salt, ½ tsp. or a bit more of pepper, ⅛ tsp. curry, and ⅛ tsp. cumin to the water in which you stew the chicken. You will not need all of the chicken for the black beans and yellow rice, and so you can use the remaining chicken to make chicken soup, adding either noodles or rice to the well-seasoned broth and thinning to the desired consistency and taste.

Black Bean Soup

1 cup dried black beans
1 medium-sized onion, diced

1 clove garlic, crushed
1 stalk of celery, chopped
1 tbsp. olive oil
½ tsp. prepared mustard
salt
pepper

Soak beans overnight. Put them in a deep kettle, cover with water, and start cooking on moderate heat. Saute onions, garlic, and celery in olive oil. Add to beans, plus the mustard. Mix thoroughly and continue cooking on low heat until beans are tender. Add more water as necessary. Season with salt and pepper, adding enough additional water to make a thick soup before serving.

Variations in ways to prepare black bean soup are many. Commonly, for example, the beans are put through a sieve or are mashed. To keep the soup thick, about 2 tbsp. of flour and 1 tbsp. of butter can be added. Before serving, the soup can be topped with slices of hard-boiled eggs and limes. A bit of sherry or rum may be stirred into the soup just before it is reheated for serving. Serves 3-4.

Cuban crackers, now available in most stores in southern Florida, should be served with this soup if possible. These crackers are also excellent with avocado dip or with the delightful guava, mango, and other fruit pastes, jams, or jellies. They complement without subtracting from flavors.

GARBANZOS

Garbanzos, also called chickpeas or Spanish beans, are used to a limited degree in the southern United States but are much more popular in the American subtropics. Most people are first introduced to garbanzos in soup, as they are the principal ingredient of Spanish bean soup, which also has many variations.

Garbanzo Soup

½ lb. dried garbanzos (2 cans garbanzos can be substituted)
1 medium-sized onion, chopped
1 cup cooked ham, diced
2 tbsp. salt pork or bacon, diced
1 large potato, diced
1 chorizo
2 tbsp. olive oil
⅛ tsp. saffron
⅛ tsp. cumin
⅛ tsp. oregano
salt
pepper
1 stalk celery, diced

If using dry garbanzos, soak overnight, then drain and cover again with fresh water. Bring to a boil, then reduce heat and simmer until garbanzos are tender. This will require at least 2 hours. Drain. If using canned garbanzos, simply drain off liquor. Saute onion and celery in olive oil. Add ham. Place garbanzos, ham, onions, celery, salt pork (or bacon), add potato in deep pan or kettle and cover with water. Add seasonings, and cook on moderate heat for 30 minutes, or until potato is done. Slice chorizo thinly and add to soup, mixing thoroughly before serving. Serves 4-6.

Marinated Garbanzos

1 large can garbanzos
3 green onions, cut crosswise including tops (or 1 small onion, diced)
2 tbsp. olive oil
1 tsp. salt
½ tsp. pepper
⅛ tsp. oregano
1 clove garlic, crushed
2 tbsp. vinegar

Drain garbanzos. Mix the oil and vinegar, adding onions, garlic, oregano, salt and pepper. Pour this mixture over garbanzos and allow them to marinate at room temperature for at least an hour. Stir several times to make certain all of the garbanzos are coated with the marinade. Chill and serve. Serves 3-4

Bean Dips

Bean dips can be made with garbanzos, pinto, Navy beans, or others.

1 can cooked beans (or 1 lb. if starting with dried beans)
1 lime
1 clove garlic, crushed
1 medium-sized onion, diced
1 tsp. salt
¼ tsp. pepper
Tabasco sauce

Place cooked beans (follow directions if using dried beans), juice of lime, and all seasonings in electric blender and make a puree. It may be necessary to add a bit of water to get blender to operate but keep mixture thick. Or beans can be mashed in a bowl or put through a ricer. Dip can be more liquid if it is to be used with thin chips, thicker if it is to be spread with a knife. Stir in 3-4 drops of Tabasco if you want to make the dip peppy.

PEANUTS

You know them best as a snack food and as peanut butter, but the versatility of the peanut is unending. George Washington Carver developed some 300 uses for peanuts, his focus on food but with oils, medicines, and other products also on his impressive list. Other uses are added regularly. Nutritionists acknowledge that the peanut is indeed one of the best sources of protein, and some say its greatest contribution will come in the next century when the peanut will help save millions from the ravages of malnutrition and starvation.

The flavorful varieties of peanuts we eat contain about 26 percent protein, making them several times richer protein sources than eggs. But some of the bland white-skinned varieties of peanuts that we do not eat contain as much as 60 percent protein. By processing these white-skinned peanuts to make flour for use as an additive to wheat flour, which has only 12 percent protein, the nutritional value of breads and other baked good can be greatly increased.

Peanuts are not true nuts, of course. They are legumes, like peas and beans, and they are produced on shrubby vinelike plants. First the plant develops yellow pealike flowers. Flowers that are fertilized wither, their stems bending down and pushing into the ground. There the pods develop. "Groundnut" is another name sometimes used for peanuts.

And peanuts did not come from Africa, as many believe. They are natives of South America where they were eaten by the Indians for centuries before the Europeans arrived. Spanish and Portuguese traders carried them to Africa and traded them for ivory, spices, and other valuables. The Africans planted the peanuts, and soon they were a staple. Slaves brought peanuts back to North America. For many years they were eaten only by the slaves and the very poor. But they were the "goober peas" that helped feed the Confederate soldiers during the Civil War. The taste for peanuts caught on! A few years later bags of roasted peanuts became popular at circuses and baseball games. In the 1890s, a doctor in St. Louis began grinding up peanuts to make peanut butter as a nutritious and easily digested food for his patients. And through the years the use of peanuts in various ways has continued to grow.

Peanuts are used mainly in cakes, cookies, and other desserts, and there are some suggestions for their use in this manner in the dessert section of

Florida is one of the largest producers of peanuts—some 150 million pounds sent to market every year.

this book. But here are a few other ways to use peanuts in your cookery. You can easily add more.

Peanut Soup

1 cup creamy peanut butter
2 qts. chicken broth
1 cup light cream
¼ cup butter
1 cup celery, sliced thinly
1 medium-sized onion, chopped
2 tbsp. flour

Melt butter in large saucepan on low heat. Add onion and celery and continue cooking until tender (but do not brown). Add flour. Stir until mixture is smooth. Add chicken broth slowly and bring to a boil. Then blend in peanut butter. Simmer for 15 minutes. Stir in cream just before serving. Serves 4-6.

Peanut Butter and Ham Spread

2 3-oz. cans of deviled ham
¼ cup peanut butter, chunky
2 tsp. prepared mustard

Put all ingredients in a bowl and mix thoroughly. Spread on bread or crackers. Serves 3-4.

Chicken with Peanut-Orange Sauce

1 fryer chicken, cut into pieces
1 tsp. salt
½ tsp. pepper
¼ tsp. garlic salt
1 tsp. paprika
2 tbsp. peanut oil
¼ cup peanut butter
1 cup orange juice

Mix salt, pepper, garlic salt, and paprika and rub onto pieces of chicken (previously washed and dried). Heat oil in skillet, add chicken, and fry until browned on all sides. Cover skillet, reduce heat, and continue to cook until chicken is tender (about 30 minutes). Put chicken on serving platter. Pour excess oil and fat from skillet. Add peanut butter and cook for several minutes. Then add orange juice and bring to a boil. Spoon this sauce over the chicken. Serves 4.

For a sauce variation, try this:

1 medium onion, chopped
1 clove garlic, minced
1 cup water
½ cup peanut butter
1 8-oz. tomato sauce
1 tbsp. sugar
1 tbsp. vinegar
1 tsp. chili powder

Cook onion and garlic in pan drippings until lightly browned. Stir in remaining ingredients gradually and continue to stir until smooth and bubbling. Put previously browned chicken in sauce and simmer until chicken is tender (about 45 minutes). Turn chicken in sauce occasionally and add more water as often as needed to keep from sticking. Also add salt to taste. Put chicken on platter and spoon remaining sauce over the top before serving.

Hamburgers Crusted with Peanuts

2 lbs. hamburger
2 eggs
1 medium-sized onion, chopped
1 clove garlic, chopped
1 tsp. salt
¼ tsp. pepper
½ cup melted butter or margarine
1 cup roasted peanuts, finely chopped
peanut oil

Mix hamburger, eggs, onion, garlic, salt, and pepper in bowl. Form into 8 hamburger patties. Brush patties on each side with butter, then put each patty in the chopped peanuts. Heat remaining butter plus peanut oil as needed in skillet and cook patties, first browning them on medium heat and then lowering heat to cook until done. Serve on buns.

Peanut Butter-Stuffed Sweet Potatoes

4 medium-sized sweet potatoes
⅔ cup milk
¼ cup peanut butter
¼ tsp. salt
⅛ tsp. pepper
⅓ cup roasted, unsalted peanuts

Bake sweet potatoes at 350 degrees for 30 minutes. Cut in half and spoon flesh out of shells. Mash. Add the milk, peanut butter, salt, and pepper. Beat until fluffy. Refill the shells and sprinkle chopped peanuts over the top. Put on cookie sheet in oven preheated to 400 degrees. Remove when top is browned. Serves 4.

Peanut Cheese Ball

1 cup roasted peanuts, chopped
¼ cup pimento, diced
½ lb. sharp cheddar cheese, grated
1 tbsp. lime juice
½ tsp. salt
1 tsp. Worcestershire sauce
1 tbsp. grated onion
⅛ tsp. cayenne

Mix all ingredients (save out half the peanuts) and shape into a ball. Coat ball with the remaining peanuts. Spread on bread or crackers.

peanuts and chicken supreme

2 chicken breasts
2 cups salted peanuts, chopped
1 cup celery, chopped
1 cup green pepper, chopped
1 tbsp. peanut oil
1 cup bean sprouts, drained
1 medium onion, chopped
3 cups rice, cooked and hot
2 tbsp. soy sauce
⅛ tsp. pepper
salt

Put celery, green pepper, onion, peanuts, and bean sprouts in bowl, then stir in soy sauce and pepper. Cube chicken breasts and simmer in peanut oil in skillet until white. Add the combined ingredients from the bowl plus 1 cup of water. Stir. Cover skillet tightly and simmer for 30 or 45 minutes. Serve over the hot rice, adding salt to taste. Serves 3-4.

CASSAVA

Cassava plants are native to Brazil but are now grown in warm climates throughout the world. They go also by such names as yucca, manioc, and others. In Florida, cassavas are grown in gardens and are sold now in many markets. Tapioca is a familiar commercial product made from the cooked, pulverized roots of a variety of cassava. If eaten raw, the starchy roots are poisonous, but the poison (hydrocyanic acid) escapes when the roots are cooked.

Cassava roots are widely used as a starchy vegetable in the areas where the plants are grown. They resemble the malanga in having small starch grains that make the cooked product more moist and slippery than white potatoes. Cassava chips, similar to potato chips, can be bought in some Florida stores that cater mainly to the Latin trade.

For cooking, the cassava roots should be peeled, cut into small pieces and boiled in salt water for at least an hour. They can then be served with salt, pepper, and butter. The cooked cassavas can also be mashed and combined with egg, flour, and a touch of baking powder to make patties that are fried in a skillet until browned on both sides. Like malangas and white potatoes, they can also be added to soups and stews.

AKEE

Akees (achees) go also by the name of "vegetable brains" in many islands of the Caribbean. The edible, nutlike portions of the fruit do have brainlike convolutions. Akees are rarely eaten in Florida, but they are popular in many parts of the West Indies, particularly in Jamaica where they are produced in large enough quantities to supply a cannery that ships to specialty food markets in the United States and elsewhere. Akees come originally from Africa.

Both the green or immature fruit and the overripe fruit are poisonous. Mature fruit can be eaten either raw or cooked. In Florida, the trees are planted mainly as ornamentals because of their attractive shape and foliage and also because of the fragrant white flowers. As people become more familiar with the akee, its use increases, both for the freshly harvested and the canned fruit. If you pick your own akees, make certain you first know how to recognize mature fruit.

Fried Akees

2 cups akees
2 tbsp. olive oil
salt
pepper

Peel akees and remove seeds. Soak for about 15 minutes in salted water (about 2 tbsp. salt per quart of water). Drain and fry in oil. Season with salt and pepper to taste. Serves 3-4.

Akees and codfish

1 lb. akees
1 lb. codfish, dried and salted
2 slices bacon, diced
1 large onion, thinly sliced
1 clove garlic, crushed
2 tomatoes, thickly sliced
salt
pepper

Soak codfish overnight. Drain and cover with fresh water. Boil fish until tender, then shred. Fry bacon until crisp. Remove from skillet and place on absorbent paper towels to save. Saute garlic in bacon grease. Reduce heat and add slices of onion, tomatoes, codfish, and akees (peeled and with seeds removed). Continue cooking for about 10 minutes, or until akees are tender. Salt and pepper to. taste. For a flavor variation, add about ⅛ tsp. thyme and 2-3 drops of Tabasco at the same time main ingredients are placed in skillet. With such variations in seasoning, this is virtually a national dish in Jamaica where the akee is most popular. Serves 4-6.

OKRA

Long popular in the southern United States, fresh okra is regularly available in the Florida winter vegetable markets. Its most common use is in soups and in the gumbos for which Creole cookery is famous. Okra is best when young and firm but still tender. Interestingly, the okra's two most familiar family relatives are cotton and hibiscus.

Fried okra

1 lb. small okra
¼ cup cornmeal
1 egg, lightly beaten
1 tsp. salt

¼ tsp. pepper
¼ cup cooking oil, or butter

Wash okra, removing stems. Cook in boiling, lightly salted water until pods are soft. Dip into egg and then into cornmeal (cracker crumbs can be used as a substitute). Fry in cooking oil or butter until brown. Serves 3-4.

Note: If the pods are large, they can be cut crosswise into slices before cooking.

Baked Okra with Tomatoes and Rice

1 lb. okra, stemmed and sliced
¼ cup rice
3 large tomatoes, peeled and sliced (or use one large can of tomatoes)
2 medium-sized onions, sliced
1 ½ tsp. salt
¼ tsp. pepper
⅛ tsp. curry
⅛ tsp. thyme
⅛ lb. butter

Grease baking dish with butter. Place layer of rice on bottom, then a layer of okra, a layer of tomatoes, and a layer of onions. Sprinkle with salt, pepper, curry, and thyme. Repeat layering until all ingredients are used. Cover and bake on low heat about 325 degrees—until rice is done. Toward end of cooking, remove the lid to brown the top. Serves 4.

Creole Gumbo

2 lbs. young okra, stemmed and sliced
1 fryer chicken
1 medium-sized onion, diced
salt
1 ½ cups cooked rice
2 tomatoes, chopped
cooking oil
pepper

Fry chicken in oil until brown. Remove chicken from frying pan and add the okra, tomato, and onion. Fry until okra is no longer "stringy." Add the chicken to the pot and season with salt and pepper to taste. Pour a quart of near-boiling water over the ingredients and cook at a moderate heat for about 45 minutes. Serve on a bed of rice in shallow soup plates. Serves 4-6.

Variations are numerous. Oyster, shrimp, crabmeat, fish flakes, or ham may be substituted for chicken, or a mixture of meats may be used. Some gumbos include at least twice as many tomatoes; others are made with lima beans. Chopped celery is a frequent addition; less commonly, potatoes, or corn. Thyme and garlic are included among the seasonings. In the West Indies, about ½ tsp. of annatto is commonly added to give coloring.

Okra and Eggplant Casserole

2 doz. small to medium okra, stemmed and sliced
1 eggplant, peeled and diced
2 tomatoes, diced
1 onion, diced
1 tbsp. butter
1 tbsp. parsley
1 tsp. salt
¼ tsp. pepper
¼ tsp. thyme

Place all vegetables in a greased casserole and stir in the seasonings.

Bake at 350 degrees for about an hour, or until vegetables are tender. If desired, casserole can be topped with grated cheese and returned to oven long enough for the cheese to melt. Serves 4-6.

Pickled Okra

>   1 ½ dozen okra (more or less, depending on how many can
>   be stored)
>   vinegar
>   peppercorns
>   dill (fresh sprigs preferred)
>   salt
>   garlic cloves
>   sugar

Wash okra and trim ends. Place in kettle and cover with lightly salted water. Bring to vigorous boil, then remove and drain. Rinse okra in cold water. Pack into jars, adding to each jar a chopped clove of garlic, 1 sprig of dill, and 2-3 peppercorns. Cover with spiced vinegar made by boiling 1 qt. of vinegar with 1 cup of sugar and 1 tbsp. of dry mustard and allowing it to cool. Refrigerate the canned okra in jars until used.

PAPAYAS

Ordinarily the papaya is considered only as a fruit in the United States, and it is treated as such in the dessert section of this book. But the papaya can also be utilized as a vegetable.

Papayas are produced on treelike herbs that have woody trunks. Some varieties may be 25–30 feet tall, but the varieties grown commercially are kept short for easier harvesting. Plants begin to produce fruit in less than a year after planting, and they may continue to be productive for as long as four years.

Papaya Greens

young papaya leaves
salt
pepper
butter

The milky sap in the leaves, stems, and skins of immature fruit contain papain, an enzyme that digests protein. This is used in commercial meat tenderizers.

Collect enough very young leaves of papayas for a "mess"—about the same quantity as for spinach or other greens. Trim off heavy stem portion and cook in boiling, salted water for about 5 minutes. Drain and repeat. Leaves should be tender, with their slight bitterness removed by the double cooking. Drain and serve with butter and a sprinkling of pepper.

Baked Papaya

2 small (grapefruit sized) green papayas
butter
1 lime
salt
pepper

Cut papayas in half and remove seeds. Slice and place in baking dish that has been greased with butter. Sprinkle each layer with lime juice, salt and pepper. Top with remaining butter. Bake at 350 degrees until tender. Serves 4, with ½ fruit for each.

Peppery Papaya Meat Sauce

1 small, still-green papaya
10-12 small red peppers
2 cloves garlic
1 large onion
4 tbsp. mustard
2 tbsp. salt
1 tsp. curry powder
1 ½ pints vinegar

Boil papaya in its skin for about 5 minutes. Cool and then cut into thin strips. Chop peppers, after removing and discarding seeds. Chop onion and garlic together until fine. Mix all ingredients in the vinegar. Heat and simmer for 20-30 minutes. Cool. Bottle and keep in the refrigerator for use as needed.

CELERY

Celery is grown in large quantities in Florida fields in winter for the vegetable markets. Though celery is one of the newest of all vegetables to be widely used, it has become one of the most common because of its versatility. It can be eaten raw, either by itself or added to salads and relishes, or it can be cooked, generally as an addition to soups and stews. Celery has skyrocketed in popularity principally since the development of pascal celeries (there are several varieties) that not only lack the bitterness that used to be a characteristic of celery but also are nearly stringless. The pascal celeries are edible from their outer stalks to their tender hearts.

Celery is included as a minor ingredient in a majority of the vegetable recipes in this book.

Fried Celery

3 cups celery, thickly diced
1 chicken bouillon cube
2 tbsp. olive oil
1 green pepper, diced
1 clove garlic, crushed
¼ tsp. thyme
1 medium-sized onion, diced
salt and pepper

Saute celery, onion, garlic, and green pepper in olive oil. Dissolve chicken bouillon cube in water, add seasonings, and pour over celery, onions, garlic, and green pepper. Cover and cook for about 20 minutes. Celery should be tender but still crisp when served. Add salt and pepper to taste before serving. Serves 3-4.

celery Soup

 2 cups celery, thinly sliced (include about 1 tbsp. of chopped
    celery leaves)
 1 medium onion, thinly sliced
 2 cups milk
 ¼ cup butter
 ¼ tsp. paprika
 2 chicken bouillon cubes
 salt
 pepper

Saute onion and celery in melted butter. Turn heat low. Dissolve bouillon cubes in 2 cups of water and add to onions and celery. Pour in milk slowly, blending with other ingredients. Continue to stir until soup thickens slightly. Add celery leaves and the salt and pepper to taste. Sprinkle paprika over the top. Serves 3-4.

Note: If a thinner soup is desired, use 1 or 2 additional bouillon cubes with additional water.

celery Stuffed with Avocado

Cut stalks of celery into pieces about 4 inches long. Fill with a thick guacamole spread (see p. 138), selecting the combination of your choice. Sprinkle with paprika.

SWEET POTATOES

Sweet potatoes (not yams) are natives of the American tropics but are now grown throughout the world. They belong to the same family as the ornamental morning glory. Sweet potatoes are grown abundantly in Florida and are common in the winter vegetable markets. Because they are so common, familiar and popular, the recipes given here are restricted to uses that might not be as well known to newcomers to Florida and the subtropics. Sweet potatoes can also be used in desserts, and these uses are described in the dessert section of this book.

Baked Sweet Potatoes in Oranges

4 sweet potatoes
4 oranges
1 tbsp. grated orange peel
¼ cup orange juice
⅛ cup sugar
salt
⅛ lb. butter
¼ cup cream

Boil sweet potatoes in lightly salted water until tender, then peel. Mash the flesh. Cut tops from oranges and hollow them by scooping out the pulp. (The needed orange juice and orange peel can be obtained at this stage of preparation.) Mix the orange juice, sugar, grated orange peel, butter, and cream with the mashed sweet potato. Mix thoroughly and then stuff into the orange shells. Place stuffed oranges on cookie sheet and bake at 375 degrees for 15 minutes. Serves 4.

Sweet Potatoes with Coconut

4 sweet potatoes
3 tbsp. freshly grated coconut
⅛ lb. butter
1 tbsp. cinnamon
½ tsp. salt
⅛ tsp. grated nutmeg

Bake sweet potatoes whole at 350 degrees for about 30 minutes (time varies with size). Cut sweet potatoes in half and remove pulp, setting skins aside. Mash sweet potatoes, mixing in butter, salt and coconut. Sprinkle cinnamon and grated nutmeg over the top. Reheat and serve. Serves 4.

Variations in stuffing include using peanuts or pecans and pineapple, either omitting coconut or in addition to coconut.

vegetables

Honey can be substituted for the sugar. The topping can be cheese or marshmallow.

Sweet Potato Croquettes

3-4 sweet potatoes
2 eggs, yolks and whites separated
½ cup flour
cooking oil
2 tbsp. lime juice
½ cup ground peanuts (or pecans or almonds)
½ tsp. salt

Boil sweet potatoes in lightly salted water until tender, then peel. Mash the sweet potatoes, adding lime juice, egg yolks, and salt. Mix until smooth and thoroughly blended. Allow to cool and then shape into croquettes. Dip first into egg whites, then into nuts, and finally into the flour. Fry in oil heated to 375 degrees until browned. Drain on paper towels before serving. Serves 3-4.

Note: Croquettes can be "peppered" by adding a dash of cayenne to the mixture, if desired. Or for an interesting variation, add 1 cup of finely ground peanuts or pecans to mixture.

Sweet Potato Soup

2-3 potatoes
2 chicken bouillon cubes
1 ½ cups milk
1 small onion, diced
1 stalk celery, finely diced
1 tsp. sugar
½ tsp. salt

Boil sweet potatoes in lightly salted water until tender. In another pan with a small amount of water, cook onion and celery until tender. Peel sweet potatoes and mash. In an electric blender (or use a beater) mix sweet potatoes, milk, chicken broth (dissolve bouillon cubes in warm or hot water), onions, celery, sugar, and salt to make a complete blend of ingredients. Reheat. Serves 3-4.

French Fried Sweet Potatoes

4-6 sweet potatoes, peeled and cut into strips
cooking oil
salt

Soak strips in salted water for about 30 minutes, then drain and dry. Fry in deep fat at 375 degrees until brown. Drain on absorbent paper towels. Sprinkle with salt before serving.

Note: Chips can also be made. Slice sweet potatoes thinly and fry in deep fat as above.

BONIATOS

Boniatos are increasing in abundance in Florida vegetable markets as a result of the greater number of residents who came originally from the Caribbean. These are large—to 4 pounds—red-skinned "potatoes" with a sweet white flesh that remains quite mealy when cooked. In this respect they resemble white potatoes and are preferred by those who find the moist, waxy texture of sweet potatoes objectionable. Also the boniato is more bland, hence it accepts all sorts of seasonings without masking them with its own flavor.

Boniatos are commonly baked or steamed. They can be substituted for either sweet potatoes or white potatoes in nearly all recipes. The result will be only slightly different because of the boniato's distinctive flavor and texture. It is highly probable that the boniato will grow in popularity as more people become acquainted with it.

Fried Boniato Croquettes

4 cups of boiled, mashed boniato
2 eggs
2 tsp. butter
1 tsp. salt

¼ *cup sugar*
¼ *tsp. cinnamon*
1 ½ *cups bread crumbs*
3 *beaten eggs*
½ *tsp. salt*

Mix mashed boniato with eggs, butter, salt, sugar, and cinnamon. Shape into nut-sized croquettes. Roll in bread crumbs, dip in salted beaten eggs, then roll in bread crumbs again. Deep-fat fry at 375 degrees until brown. Drain on paper towels. Should make 12 or more croquettes.

Baked Boniatos

4 medium boniatos (baked potato size)
butter
cinnamon
sugar

Put washed boniatos in oven preheated to 375 degrees and cook for 1 hour or until soft. Split boniatos, sprinkle with sugar and cinnamon, top with two patties of butter (or equivalent). Serves 4.

TOMATOES

Tomatoes, like so many other common vegetables, are so well known and have so many uses that their inclusion in this book seems almost unnecessary. It is worth noting, however, that the tomato is a native of Peru, where two kinds were known—one producing round, red cherry-like fruit and the other slightly larger, yellow, pear-shaped fruits. They were discovered by Spanish explorers who first took them to Europe as ornamental curios rather than food. It was many years before their use as food spread through Europe, and it has been only recently that the tomato has been widely accepted. Who could now imagine Italian cuisine without tomatoes? Or any kind of cooking?

Florida's crop of tomatoes is harvested from autumn through early spring. In many areas, people are invited into the field to pick their own. The use of tomatoes in Florida and the subtropics does not differ greatly from the ways they are used elsewhere, though what accompanies them might be quite different from what the visitor or new resident has known before.

Tomato and Avocado

> 1 tomato per person
> 1 avocado, peeled and mashed
> 1 onion, diced
> 1-2 stalks of celery, diced
> 1 lime
> salt
> pepper
> paprika

Peel tomatoes, remove cores, and scoop out most of pulp. Stuff the cavity with diced celery and onions, seasoning with salt and pepper. Squeeze lime juice over the mashed avocado (equivalent of about 2 tsp. of juice should be enough) and mix. Spoon the mashed avocado onto the top of each tomato. Sprinkle with paprika.

Tomatoes and Oranges

> 1 small tomato per person
> 1 orange per person
> 1 head of lettuce
> paprika
> mayonnaise (or comparable creamy salad dressing)
> chopped pecans or peanuts

Place thick slices of lettuce or several thickness of leaves in the bottom of each individual salad bowl or plate. Put a layer of tomato slices on the lettuce, then a layer of orange slices. Repeat. Mix nuts with salad dressing and spread over the orange slices. Sprinkle with paprika.

Stuffed Baked Tomatoes

1 large tomato per person
1 onion, diced
1 green pepper, diced
1 stalk celery, chopped
½ cup chopped chicken, ham, or shrimp
¼ cup bread crumbs
2 tbsp. olive oil
⅛ tsp. oregano
⅛ tsp. thyme
salt
pepper

Cut stem end from each tomato and scoop out seeds and pulp. Saute onions, green pepper, and celery in olive oil. Add bread crumbs and tomato pulp. Sprinkle with oregano and thyme and season to taste with salt and pepper. Add the chicken, ham, or shrimp. Mix thoroughly. Stuff mixture into tomato shells, heaping on top. Bake at 375 degrees for 25 minutes.

Stuffed Raw Tomatoes

1 tomato per person
1-2 stalks of celery, diced
1 medium-sized onion, diced
1 cup cooked chicken, diced (or shrimp, tuna, or ham)
1 green pepper, diced
1 head of lettuce
1 small cucumber, diced
2 hardcooked eggs, sliced
French dressing (or an olive oil-vinegar mixture)
salt and pepper

Cut stem end from each tomato. Scoop out seeds and most of the pulp. Mix celery, onions, green pepper, and chicken (or other meat), stirring in the French dressing and adding salt and pepper to taste. Fill cavities of tomatoes with this mixture and top with a slice of

171

hardboiled egg. Serve on a lettuce leaf and surround with any of the mixture that remains. (Quantities of various ingredients will naturally vary with the size of tomatoes and the number being stuffed; the above proportions should be adequate for 4–6 tomatoes.)

Herbed Tomatoes

4-6 medium to large tomatoes, peeled and cored
¼ cup celery, finely chopped
2 tbsp. parsley, finely chopped
1 small onion, finely chopped
¼ cup butter or margarine
1 ½ tsp. brown sugar
1 tsp. salt
¼ tsp. pepper
½ tsp. oregano

Melt butter or margarine in skillet. Add brown sugar, salt, pepper, and the tomatoes, the core side down. Cover and simmer for 5 minutes. Turn tomatoes, spooning butter mixture over the top. Add all remaining ingredients to sauce and simmer uncovered for additional 5 minutes. Spoon sauce over tomatoes before serving. Serves 4–6.

Fried Green Tomatoes

1-2 tomatoes per person
1 tbsp. flour per tomato
cooking oil
1 egg
salt
pepper

Cut tomatoes into thick slices. Mix flour, egg, salt, and pepper. Dip slices of tomato into this mixture. Fry in oil until browned on each side.

EGGPLANT

Eggplants, which belong to the same plant family as tomatoes and white potatoes, came from southern Asia but have been in cultivation for centuries. Their name came from the egg-sized fruit that were produced originally on the plants. Some were yellow, others were white or brown, and some were round or oval. During the many years of cultivation and the spread of eggplants around the world, the large dark-purple fruit that we know today were developed.

Eggplants are obtained fresh in Florida's winter vegetable markets, but many people prefer to grow their own. It requires only a few plants to keep a family well supplied. Eggplants are familiar and popular in the Caribbean, and on many islands they go by their French name, aubergine.

Fried Eggplant

   2 medium-sized eggplants
   ¼ cup bread crumbs
   2 eggs, beaten
   ¼ cup cooking oil
   1 tsp. salt
   ¼ tsp. pepper

Peel eggplants and slice (½ inch thick). Salt each slice lightly and place in a bowl. After about an hour, pour off any liquid that has been drawn out by the salt, and dry each slice. Dip each slice first into the egg and then into the bread crumbs. Fry in hot oil until brown on each side. Season with salt and pepper before serving. Serves 4-6.

Eggplant with Tomatoes, Green Peppers, and Celery

   2 eggplants, peeled and cubed
   3 tomatoes, peeled and chopped

3 stalks celery, diced
⅛ tsp. thyme
salt
2 onions, diced
1 green pepper, diced
2 tbsp. olive oil (or other cooking oil)
pepper

Salt eggplant cubes and allow to stand for at least half an hour, then drain off liquid and dry cubes. Saute tomatoes, green pepper, celery, and onions in olive oil. Reduce heat. Add thyme and salt and pepper to taste. Add eggplant cubes to other vegetables. Cover and cook on medium to low heat, stirring regularly, until eggplant is tender. Add more salt and pepper if needed. Serves 4-6.

Stuffed Eggplant

2 eggplants
4 slices bacon, diced
½ cup celery, chopped
2 cups bread crumbs
salt
1 cup crushed pineapple
2 tbsp. butter
¼ cup chopped cashews
1 egg
pepper

Stem or boil unpeeled eggplant until tender, requiring about 20 minutes. Cut eggplants in half carefully so that skin remains intact. Scoop out most of the pulp, leaving about ½-inch thickness. Cut removed pulp into small pieces. Fry bacon until about half done, then add eggplant and celery to skillet. Continue cooking until eggplant is browned. Stir in the nuts, bread crumbs, and well beaten egg. Mix thoroughly, adding salt and pepper to taste. Stuff eggplant shells with this mixture, top with crushed pineapple, and bake at 350 degrees for about 30 minutes. Serves 4.

cold Eggplant Salad

1 large eggplant
2 tsp. lime juice
1 cup celery, diced
½ cup chopped pecans (cashews, walnuts, or other)
French dressing
1 small onion, diced
salt and pepper

Peel and cube eggplant. Cook cubes in lightly salted water to which lime juice has been added. When cubes are tender, drain and cool. Mix cooked eggplants with onions, nuts, and celery adding a coating of French dressing as the mixing is done. Serve on lettuce leaf as a salad. Hardboiled eggs, sliced or quartered, make a good companion and an attractive garnish.

Eggplant Fritters

1 large eggplant
2 eggs beaten
¼ tsp. pepper
½ cup cracker crumbs
1 tsp. salt

Boil unpeeled eggplant until tender. Cut in half and remove the pulp. Mash and allow to cool. Stir in eggs, salt, pepper, and cracker crumbs, adding more if necessary to make the mixture stiff. Drop by the spoonful into deep fat at 375 degrees. Remove when brown and drain on absorbent paper towels. Serves 3-4.

Eggplant Stuffed with Hamburger

2 eggplants
¾ lb. hamburger
1 onion, diced
1 green pepper, diced
1 cup cooked rice
⅛ tsp. thyme

2 tbsp. olive oil (or other cooking oil)
1 clove garlic, crushed
1 ½ tsp. salt
¼ tsp. pepper
Tabasco

Cut eggplants in half and scoop them out, leaving ¼ to ½ inches to edge. Cook hamburger, onions, and peppers in oil. When hamburger is about half cooked, add the chopped-up eggplant removed from the halves. Season with thyme, salt, pepper, and 3-4 drops of Tabasco. Continue cooking until eggplant is tender. Add cooked rice and mix thoroughly. Put eggplant shells in greased baking dish and stuff them with the hamburger-rice mixture. Bake in oven at 350 degrees for about 40 minutes.

Note: Parmesan cheese can be sprinkled over the top before placing in oven. Serves 4.

Eggplant and Chicken in a Skillet

2-3 lb. frying chicken, cut into serving portions
1 medium-sized eggplant, peeled and diced
1 onion, chopped
2 tomatoes, peeled and diced
butter or margarine
½ cup chicken broth
paprika
1 clove garlic, crushed
2 tsp. salt
¼ tsp. pepper
2 tbsp. butter
¼ tsp. thyme
1 tbsp. parsley, chopped

Sprinkle chicken with paprika, 1 tsp. of salt and ¼ tsp. pepper. Melt butter or margarine in large skillet. Add chicken and brown lightly. Remove from skillet. Add the broth, scraping the brown particles from bottom of skillet into the broth. Add garlic, eggplant, onion, and tomato. Sprinkle with remaining salt and the thyme and parsley. Arrange pieces of chicken on top of this mixture in the skillet. Cover and simmer for 30 minutes. Serves 4-6.

WHITE POTATOES

The white potato is the most frequently used vegetable in temperate regions of Europe and North America. In most of Asia, rice is the principal source of starch rather than potatoes. In the tropics, cassavas, malangas, and other starchy roots take the place of potatoes when rice is not used. Everywhere, the overlaps are increasing as people and their cultures become more intermixed.

Florida produces great quantities of potatoes for the winter markets. These fresh new potatoes can be bought at roadside markets or from packing houses. They help make many Florida fresh vegetable meals more memorable.

Potato Pancakes

4-6 potatoes, peeled
1 egg
1 tbsp. flour
cooking oil
¼ tsp. baking powder
1 tsp. salt
¼ tsp. pepper

Grate raw potatoes finely and mix with egg, flour, baking powder, salt, and pepper. Add a very small amount of water or milk if necessary to make mixture smooth. Spoon onto a hot griddle in pancake-size portions and flatten with a spatula. Brown on one side, then turn. Serves 3-4.

For a variation add 1 medium-sized onion, diced, to the pancake mixture. Or if fritters are preferred to pancakes, keep the mixture thick, and drop by the spoonful into deep fat.

Potato Soup

3 potatoes, diced
1 ½ pints of milk
2 tbsp. chopped chives or green onion tops
butter
salt
pepper

Cook potatoes in lightly salted water. Drain. Add to milk, with salt and pepper to taste. Heat, dotting surface with butter and sprinkling with chopped chives or green onion tops before serving. Serves 3-4. For a smooth soup, put cooked potatoes and milk in blender before heating.

GREEN PEPPERS

Like both tomatoes and potatoes, peppers were one of the discoveries made by Spanish explorers in the New World. They had long been cultivated by the Indians, with virtually every variety known today already developed. The explorers called them peppers because the hot kinds were so spicy, like the prized sought-after black pepper of the East Indies.

Sweet peppers can be eaten raw, either alone or in salads. When mature, they are commonly preserved by sweet pickling. Peppers are added to meat loaf, stews, and sauces, or they are stuffed themselves with a variety of meat and rice dishes

Fresh green peppers are abundantly available at Florida vegetable markets. They can also be grown on small garden plots, the plants continuing to bear over a long period.

Peppers and Rice

3 green peppers, chopped
1 onion, chopped
½ lb. rice
⅛ tsp. thyme

2 tbsp. butter
2 cups chicken broth
salt
pepper

Fry onions and green peppers lightly in butter. Add rice, thyme, salt, and pepper. Pour chicken broth over the mixture and cook on medium heat until rice is done. Stir several times and also add water if necessary. Serves 3-4. Note: A small amount of curry (¼ to ½ tsp. depending on taste) can be stirred into the rice as it is cooking.

Peppers Stuffed with Shrimp

1 large green pepper per person (ingredients here are for 4)
1 ¼ cups cooked macaroni
½ cup cooked shrimp, cut into small pieces
¼ cup grated cheese
½ tsp. salt
⅛ tsp. pepper
¼ cup French dressing

Slice tops from pepper and remove seeds. Parboil peppers for about 3 minutes, then drain. Stuff with the well-mixed shrimp, macaroni, French dressing, salt, and pepper. Cover top with grated cheese and place in greased baking dish in oven at 375 degrees for about 25 minutes.

Note: Stuffing can be varied greatly. Hamburger, tomato, and rice is common. Chicken and rice or ham and rice are also good.

Green Pepper and Tuna Casserole

1 green pepper, diced
¼ lb. broken spaghetti
2 cans of tuna (7 oz. each)
1 onion, diced
1 can mushroom soup

1 small can (4 oz.) mushrooms, sliced or pieces
1 cup grated cheddar cheese
salt
pepper

Cook spaghetti, drain, and place in greased casserole. Add the green pepper, mushroom soup, onion, tuna, and about half of the cheese. Mix thoroughly, with salt and pepper to taste. Spread remainder of cheese over the top. Place in oven at 375 degrees and cook for about 40 minutes. Serves 3-4

HOT PEPPERS

Many kinds of hot peppers are grown in Florida and the Caribbean for use mainly in sauces. Small amounts are added to stews, soups, dips, and other dishes to give them a spicy zip. Some are used fresh; others are dried and then used as needed.

Some kinds of hot peppers are slim and pencil-like. Others are round like cherries; still others are shaped like strawberries. Hot peppers also range in size from only an inch or two long or not larger than cherries to some that are the size and shape of bananas. Perhaps the best and briefest recommendation for how to use hot peppers is sparingly. For those who do like "fire" for their food, however, a good peppersauce does add pep without necessarily killing the flavor.

Simple Peppersauce

8-10 hot peppers
vinegar

Fill vinegar cruet (or similar container) loosely with peppers. Pour vinegar over them and allow to stand for several days before using. Only the vinegar is used, the peppers remaining in the container. More vinegar can be added as the original supply is utilized. Replace the peppers when the sauce begins to lose its zip.

Note: If the container has a sprinkle-type top so that solids are held back, the peppersauce can be given additional distinctiveness by adding a bay leaf, 4-6 whole cloves, and a clove of garlic cut into several pieces.

CUCUMBERS

This "cool" vegetable has a surprising number of uses. A member of the squash or gourd family, along with watermelons, the cucumber has been cultivated for so many centuries that its precise origin is no longer known. The cucumber was a favorite of both the Greeks and the Romans, but it was well known in China much earlier, probably originating in southern Asia. Cucumbers are eaten mainly raw, either as the main component of a salad or as an ingredient with other vegetables. Fewer people know that the cucumber can also be cooked—boiled briefly in salted water until just tender and then served with sour cream or Hollandaise sauce. Or they can be French fried—cut into strips, dipped into a batter of cracker crumbs and eggs, and then fried in oil at 375 degrees until golden brown.

Like many other common vegetables, cucumbers are produced in abundance in Florida during the winter. Residents can take advantage of their availability at local markets and can often buy culls at bargain prices.

Gazpacho

2 cucumbers, peeled and cut into chunks
4 tomatoes, peeled and chopped
2 green peppers, chopped
1 bunch green onions, chopped (or 1 large onion, chopped)
2 sprigs fresh parsley
½ tsp. pepper
1 ½ tsp. salt
⅛ tsp. cayenne pepper
⅛ tsp. cumin
1 clove garlic, crushed

1 can (12 oz.) tomato juice
¼ cup olive oil
¼ cup vinegar

Puree vegetables, including onion and garlic, in electric blender or use fine grinder. Add seasonings, vinegar, oil, and tomato juice. Mix thoroughly. Chill and serve. This is a delightfully refreshing cold soup for a hot day. Serves 4-6.

Note: There are numerous variations in the preparation of gazpacho, both in the seasonings and in the proportions of the vegetables. The can be developed to satisfy individual tastes. If the olive oil is objectionable, as it is to some people, substitute 1 can of beef bouillon diluted with ½ can of water. If the soup is too spicy, use no cayenne. Gazpacho is literally a liquid salad that can be eaten with a spoon or drunk.

Cucumber Dip

2 cucumbers, peeled
¼ cup olive oil
1 tbsp. vinegar
¼ cup English walnuts
1 clove garlic
½ tsp. salt
⅛ tsp. pepper

Grind cucumbers or chop them very fine, but small pieces should be identifiable as cucumbers. Pulverize the garlic and walnuts; this can be done in an electric blender, using the vinegar as the liquid vehicle. Mix all ingredients in a bowl. Adjust salt and pepper to taste. The result should be a "chunky" liquid that can be picked up easily with chips or crackers.

Cucumbers and Onions

3 cucumbers, peeled and sliced
1 large onion, sliced thinly
¼ cup vinegar

1 ½ tsp. salt
½ tsp. sugar

Put cucumbers and onions in bowl. Mix while sprinkling with the sugar, salt, and pepper. Pour vinegar (which can be diluted with about ½ water if desired) over the top of cucumbers and onions, then mix thoroughly.

For a variation, use lime juice rather than vinegar.

Cucumbers Cooked with Tomatoes and Green Peppers

3-4 cucumbers, peeled and diced
2-3 tomatoes, chopped
1 green pepper, diced
1 large onion, diced
1 cup chicken broth
1 clove garlic
1 tsp. salt
¼ tsp. pepper
2 tsp. olive oil

Saute onion and garlic in oil in saucepan. Add chicken broth, tomatoes, cucumbers, and green pepper, plus salt and pepper. Cover and cook on low heat for 20-25 minutes. Serves 3-4.

CHAYOTES

Called cho-chos in Jamaica and other parts of the Caribbean, chayotes were cultivated in the American tropics before the arrival of the Europeans. They are believed to be the oldest of all cultivated squashes. From their native land, chayotes have now been spread to warm regions throughout the world. Though they have been grown in limited quantities in Florida for many years, their popularity has only recently climbed, due mainly to the greater number of people from the American subtropics now living in Florida. Chayotes are now seen regularly in Florida markets.

Chayotes are easily grown by the home gardener, too. The vine will quickly take over a fence, an old tree snag, or a trellis. It will produce chayotes year around.

Left on the vine, if it is growing in rich, moist soil, a chayote becomes quite large—as much as 10 inches long and as big around as a grapefruit. It has several deep furrows on its sides, and the skin is light green (mottled or white in some varieties). The seed of large, mature fruit may sprout while the chayote is still attached to the vine. Planted with the sprout up, a new vine is quickly in the making.

Very young, egg-sized chayotes have a tender skin and do not have to be peeled before they are cooked. They can also be eaten raw, sliced thinly and added to tossed salads. As the chayotes mature, the skin becomes thicker and tougher. For baking, the skin is left on, forming an excellent shell for the cooked squash. For other uses, the chayote is peeled. Inside is a single, very large seed that is not removed. It is eaten with the pulp in whatever way it is cooked. Like other squash, the chayote can be utilized both as a vegetable and as a dessert. Sugar makes the difference.

Those who grow their own chayotes soon learn also that the tender young shoots that sprout up from the base of the old vine or from mature fruit that drop can be eaten as greens. After several years, too, the base of the mature plant develops a large, round tuber—to as big as a dishpan. This is also edible—peeled and cooked in lightly salted water until tender, then served with butter, salt, and pepper.

Chayotes have a distinctive, though bland flavor. They "take on" the flavor of seasonings or of other vegetables with which they are cooked. Cut into slices or bite-sized chunks they can be added to soups and stews.

Steamed Chayotes

4-6 chayotes, peeled and sliced
butter
pepper
salt

Steam slices of chayote until tender. About 15 minutes generally suffices. Place chayotes in bowl and add salt and pepper to taste. Put several chunks of butter on the steaming-hot vegetable just before serving.

Fried Chayote

4-6 chayotes, peeled and sliced
2 tbsp. olive oil (or other cooking oil)
salt
pepper

Fry slices in oil until browned on both sides. Salt and pepper to taste.

Chayote Medley

3-4 medium-sized chayotes, peeled and sliced thinly
1 medium onion, sliced and separated into rings
4-5 tomatoes, cut into wedges
1 green pepper cut into chunks
1 ½ tsp. garlic salt
1 tsp. sugar
1 tsp. pepper
½ cup olive oil

Mix the vegetables and seasoning. Saute in oil until lightly brown.

Chayote slices will take on flavor of seasonings but will still be crisp. Serves 3-4.

Baked Chayote

4-6 large chayotes
¾ lb. hamburger
1 tomato, chopped
1 onion, diced
½ cup cooked rice
2 tbsp. olive oil
⅛ tsp. oregano
¼ cup grated cheese
cayenne pepper
1 clove garlic, crushed

Cut chayotes in half and steam them or boil in lightly salted water until tender. Be careful not to cook too long; about 15 minutes should be adequate. Remove cooked pulp carefully and set shells aside. Fry hamburger in olive oil, adding oregano, tomatoes, onion, and garlic. Keep heat low after cooking is in process. When mixture is cooked, add rice and chayote pulp. Stir thoroughly, salting and peppering to taste. A dash of cayenne will give the mixture pep. Fill chayote shells with this mixture, sprinkling the grated cheese over the top of each. Bake at 350 degrees for about 20 minutes. Serves 3-4.

Note: Ham, shrimp, chicken—almost any meat or seafood can be substituted for the hamburger.

Chayote Pancakes

4 cups cooked (steamed) chayote, mashed and run through
    colander
1 egg, lightly beaten
3 tbsp. milk
1 ½ tbsp. flour
1 tsp. baking powder
1 ½ tsp. salt

Mix all ingredients thoroughly. Fry on griddle like pancakes or drop by spoonful into hot fat and cook until brown, like fritters. Can be eaten with salt and pepper or with syrup.

YELLOW SQUASH

These small crooknecked squash are abundant in the Florida winter vegetable market and have the same widely varied utility as most squash. Young, unpeeled squash are most commonly steamed until tender, then served with salt, pepper, and ample amounts of butter. They can also be combined with other vegetables in stews and soups. If you grow your own squash, you can enjoy a real delight: fried flowers. To serve 3 or 4 people, collect about two dozen flowers. Wash them (to get rid of insects inside), then fry them in a skillet in butter, or they can be dipped in an egg batter and deep-fat fried. Season with salt and serve immediately. Flowers of pumpkins, zucchini, and other squash are equally good. Dip in powdered sugar if you want them as a dessert snack.

Stuffed Yellow Squash

6 large yellow squash
2 slices bacon, diced
¼ lb. hamburger
1 small onion, diced
1 small green pepper, diced
½ cup cooked rice
1 small tomato, chopped
¼ cup grated cheddar cheese
salt
pepper

Wash squash carefully to keep soft skins intact. Boil in lightly salted water until the squash begin to soften. Remove, drain, and cut in half lengthwise. Scoop out pulp carefully. Set shells aside, and save pulp in bowl. Fry bacon on medium heat, adding hamburger when the bacon is about half cooked. When hamburger begins to brown, add onion, green pepper, tomato, and pulp removed from squash. Mix thoroughly and continue cooking on moderate heat until done. Stir in the cooked rice and add salt and pepper to taste. Stuff squash shells carefully with this mixture. Remember, these squash are soft; be gentle. Spread grated cheese over the top and bake at 350 degrees for about 15 minutes. Serves 3-4.

peppered Squash

8-12 medium-sized yellow squash, washed and sliced

1 onion, diced

2-3 hot peppers

2 tbsp. butter

¼ cup grated cheese

salt

pepper

Cook squash, tomatoes, and onions in oil in covered skillet until tender. Stir several times. Salt and pepper to taste, then add hot peppers (these can be cut into thirds) and place in a greased casserole, sprinkling the grated cheese over the top. Bake in oven at 350 degrees for about 15 minutes. Serves 3-4.

Note: For a variation and complete-meal casserole, add cooked, chopped ham (about ½ cup) to casserole. If hot peppers are objectionable, they can be omitted.

ZUCCHINI

Among the other soft-shelled squash commonly seen in Florida are cocozelles, zucchinis, and pattypans (scallop). Of these, the zucchini is most distinctive, seeming to demand an Italian or Greek treatment in its preparation. It is perfectly adaptable, as are the others, to other squash recipes, however.

zucchinis and corn

2 medium-sized zucchinis, washed and sliced

4 ears of corn

1 onion, diced

3 tomatoes, peeled and chopped

1 green pepper, diced

2 tbsp. olive oil

1 ½ tsp. salt

½ tsp. sugar

¼ tsp. pepper

⅛ tsp. oregano

¼ cup seasoned croutons

Cut corn from cobs and mix with zucchinis in greased casserole. Add other ingredients, including seasonings, and mix thoroughly. Bake in oven at 350 degrees for 20 minutes. Remove and sprinkle croutons over top. Return to oven for about 5 additional minutes. Serves 6.

sweet and sour zucchini

4 cups zucchini, sliced

1 cup celery, sliced

2 tomatoes, peeled and cut into eighths

¼ cup vinegar

1 small onion, finely diced

1 clove garlic, crushed

½ cup water

2 tbsp. olive oil

3 tsp. cornstarch

1 tbsp. sugar

2 tsp. prepared mustard

¾ tsp. salt

⅛ tsp. pepper

In skillet, stir together the oil, cornstarch, sugar, onion, mustard, salt, garlic, and pepper. Add water and vinegar. Cook on medium heat until mixture thickens and begins to boil. Add the zucchini and the celery. Cover and cook for 8-10 minutes, or until vegetables are tender but still crisp. Stir occasionally while cooking. Add tomatoes and cook for additional 2-3 minutes or until heated through. Serves 4-6.

CALABAZA

Newcomers to Florida and the Caribbean will probably see calabazas for the first time, though they are shipped to some northern markets. The calabaza is a hard-shelled squash that is cooked as a vegetable like the more familiar and smaller butternut, acorn, and similar kinds of squash. Most commonly, these squash are baked. Cooked, mashed calabazas are mixed with eggs, a small amount of baking powder, diced onion, salt, and pepper and then spooned into deep fat to make fritters. Because of the pumpkinlike flesh and flavor, calabazas are used also in making pies. They can be steamed until the flesh is tender, then served hot with salt, pepper, and butter. A popular marinade among people of Cuban descent is made by crushing 4-6 cloves of garlic and adding to hot cooking oil. After about a minutes, ½ cup of lime juice is added. This mixture is poured over cooked cubes of calabaza. Cold slices are combined with lettuce and seasoned with salt, pepper, and vinegar.

As long as a calabaza is kept cool and out of the sun, it will keep for a long time. Most of those seen on the market are about the size of coconuts, but they get several times larger if left on the vines to mature. The thick rind is a light yellowish-green, mottled with dark green. The flesh is orange-yellow.

Calabazas Stuffed with Sausage and Beef

    1 calabaza (coconut size)
    ¾ lb. pork sausage
    ¾ lb. hamburger

1 large onion, chopped
1 green pepper, chopped
2 cloves garlic, crushed
1 cup cooked rice
1 tsp. oregano
1 tsp. thyme
2 tsp. salt
1 tsp. pepper
Tabasco

Cut a lidlike top from the calabaza and save. With spoon, remove seeds, cleaning out the inside of the calabaza. Simmer calabaza in lightly salted water until the flesh is tender. Drain and dry the outside shell. Fry sausage, pouring off excess grease and adding hamburger, onion, green pepper, oregano, and thyme when the sausage is about half cooked. Cook on medium heat until the sausage and hamburger mixture is fully cooked. Stir in rice, and season mixture with salt and pepper plus 3-4 drops of Tabasco. Stuff scooped out shell of calabaza with this mixture, packing it in firmly. Place lid on calabaza, and bake at 350 degrees for about 40 minutes. Cool slightly, then serve by slicing squash and spooning some of the stuffing mixture into the center of the slice on a plate. Serves 4-6.

Note: This same stuffing can be used for acorn and other squash.

LETTUCE AND OTHER SALAD GREENS

Florida's winter vegetable markets are filled with a variety of fresh, locally grown lettuce for combining with the fruits and vegetables of the subtropics in healthful, superbly tasty salads. Those who have the space and the inclination to do so can also grow their own. Fresh garden lettuce for Christmas is a great treat.

The kinds available include both leaf lettuce and head lettuce.

Nearly all of the endive and escarole sold in vegetable markets throughout the country comes from Florida. Also available for salads is Chinese cabbage, fresh spinach, red and green cabbage, and the flavorful though less commonly used tops of mustard, beets, turnips, kale, and collards. At least a portion of these greens mixed with lettuce makes a salad distinctive. From November through April or early May in Florida, greens are plentiful. This is a special delight for those interested in low calorie foods that are high in minerals and vitamins.

Before you store lettuce in your refrigerator for later use, sort over it and eliminate any leaves that would have to be thrown away later anyhow. Wash the lettuce and then drain it, shaking off all the excess moisture. Then place it in a plastic bag. In this way, the lettuce is ready for immediate use. Very important for salads, it will be cool, crisp, and dry. The dryness will help in coating the leaves with dressings, which cannot cling to and thus flavor leaves that are moist.

Lettuce is used almost totally in salads or sandwiches and is eaten raw. For those who have never eaten wilted lettuce, the following may add a new dimension to their meals.

Wilted Lettuce

2 heads leaf lettuce
1 large onion, chopped (or better, 6-8 chopped green onions, including tops)
4 slices bacon, diced
¼ cup vinegar
2 tbsp. lime juice
1 tsp. sugar
1 ½ tsp. salt
½ tsp. pepper

Fry bacon, remove from skillet and dry on paper towels. Pour off about a third of the bacon drippings. Add vinegar and lime juice to the bacon drippings and bring to a boil. Add onions, sugar, salt, and pepper. Reduce heat. Cut lettuce into bite-sized pieces. Pour the hot vinegar mixture over the lettuce in a bowl and mix thoroughly. Top with the crisp bacon. Note: The above can be made in smaller quantities by reducing proportions. Also, spinach and various other green can be prepared in this manner.

4.

Meats & Poultry

The basic ways meats are cooked are the same in Florida and the Caribbean as elsewhere. The differences are mainly in seasonings and sauces and in the companions that make the meal. The few recipes here are offered to give a new flair to some old favorites.

Bahamian Chicken

1 chicken, roasting size
1 package seasoned bread crumbs (or loaf of stale bread)
2 tomatoes, diced
3 large potatoes, peeled and quartered
1 onion diced
butter or margarine
salt
pepper
1 ½ cups water

Mix the bread crumbs or stuffing and the diced onion with melted butter, 2 tsp. salt, and dash of pepper. Dry inside cavity of chicken and stuff lightly with this mixture. Place chicken in baking pan, spreading butter over surface and sprinkling with thyme, salt, and pepper. Place the potatoes, tomatoes, and the remaining bread crumbs around the chicken. Pour in water. Bake at 400 degrees for about an hour, or until chicken is tender. Serves 4.

Spiced Marinated Chicken

2 chickens, broiling size cut in half
2 hot peppers, finely diced (or 1 tsp. cayenne pepper)
1 large onion, sliced thinly and separated into rings
1 green pepper, cut in rings
1 tbsp. paprika
3 tsp. salt
½ tsp. pepper
1 ½ tsp. olive oil
1 cup lime juice

Rub halves of chickens with olive oil, then sprinkle with paprika, salt and pepper. Place chicken in shallow pan and pour over them the ½ cup of lime juice to which the diced hot peppers have been added. Cover and place in refrigerator for at least eight hours, turning chicken several times and spooning the liquid over them. Broil the chicken halves (this can be done in a oven or on an outdoor grill) until done. Saute onion rings in small amount of oil, adding the green pepper rings and the remaining lime juice, salt, and pepper. Spoon this mixture onto the chicken in shallow baking pan and place in oven at 350 degrees. Serve as soon as chicken is heated through again. Serves 4-6.

Chicken Cooked in Coconut

2 coconuts, medium-sized
1 chicken, boned and diced
1 onion, diced
1 green pepper, diced
3 slices of bacon, diced
1 clove garlic, crushed
1 tbsp. brown sugar
1 bay leaf
salt and pepper
Tabasco
2 tbsp. rum

Put bacon in frying pan on medium heat. When bacon is cooked tender and not crisp, add chicken and fry until done. Remove chicken and bacon. Add the onion, green pepper, and garlic to skillet and cook until tender, then return chicken and bacon to skillet. Add brown sugar and pepper, plus 2-3 drops of Tabasco. Cut tops from coconuts at about level of "eyes" and save for lids. Pour out liquid and wash coconuts thoroughly on outside. Fill each coconut with chicken, adding ½ bay leaf to each and 1 tbsp. rum. Replace lids and put coconuts in baking pan in oven at 350 degrees for an hour. Serve in coconuts. Serves 4-6.

Limed Chicken

   3 fryer-sized chickens, cut into serving pieces
   6-8 limes, juice of
   1 ½ cups flour
   1 cup cornmeal
   1 clove garlic, crushed
   ¾ lb. butter or margarine
   salt
   pepper

Add garlic and 2 tsp. of salt to lime juice. Pour this mixture over the pieces of chicken in a bowl. Marinate in the refrigerator for at least an hour, turning several times. Mix the flour and cornmeal, adding 1 tsp. salt and 1/2 tsp. pepper. Heat butter in skillet. Coat each piece of chicken with flour and cornmeal and fry until brown. Add additional butter if needed. Serves 4-6.

To make a complete meal of limed chicken, place cooked pieces in a large deep skillet and surround them with tomatoes (2, cut into wedges), 1 stalk of diced celery, 1 tbsp. of raisins, and 1 cup of fresh, cubed pineapples. Add about ¾ cup of water, cover, and cook on medium heat until tomatoes are done. This can be served with rice that has been cooked with about ⅛ tsp. of saffron to give it color and about ⅛ tsp. of curry to add a distinctive flavor These seasonings are optional.

Chicken and Garbanzos

2 small fryer chickens, cut into serving pieces
2 tomatoes, cut into wedges
1 large onion, chopped
2 cloves garlic, crushed
Tabasco
¼ cup olive oil
1 can garbanzos (dried can be used, requiring overnight soaking
    and cooking)
salt
pepper

Saute onions and garlic in oil, then remove. Add chicken to oil and cook until browned. Mix the onions, garlic, garbanzos, and tomatoes with the chicken. Season with salt, pepper, and several drops of Tabasco. Cover, reducing the heat to medium-low and cooking until chicken is tender. Serves 3-4.

Chicken Gumbo with Oysters

1 stewing chicken
1 lb. stewing beef
2 doz. oysters, shucked
1 ½ cups okra, diced

2 tomatoes, coarsely diced
1 onion, diced
1 tbsp. butter or margarine
1 bay leaf
salt
pepper

Cut chicken into serving pieces and place in kettle with beef, tomatoes, and okra. Cover with water. Heat to boiling, then reduce heat to medium and cook until beef and chicken are tender. Remove bones from chicken and cut beef into small, bite-sized pieces. Add oyster and bay leaf. Salt and pepper to taste. Cook on low heat for about 20 minutes, or until edges of oysters begin to curl. Serves 4-6.

chicken with pork

1 chicken (3-4 lbs.) cut into serving pieces
2 lbs. pork, with some fat, cut into cubes
½ cup lime juice
2 cloves garlic, crushed
2 ½ tbsp. soy sauce
¼ tsp. pepper
2 tbsp. olive oil or other cooking oil

Place lime juice, garlic, soy sauce, and pepper in saucepan. Add the chicken and pork. Heat to boiling, then simmer until meat is tender, adding additional water if necessary. Drain meat, saving broth. Saute meat in hot oil until browned, then return it to the liquid in the saucepan. Heat for serving, adding more salt and pepper if necessary.

Beef Rolls

2 lbs. steak, at least ½ inch thick (chuck steak will do)
1 large onion, chopped
2 tomatoes, chopped
1 chayote, diced

1 egg, lightly beaten

1 clove garlic, crushed

1 slice of bacon for each roll

¼ cup bread crumbs

¼ cup tomato sauce

1 tbsp. Worcestershire sauce

¼ cup lime juice

1 tbsp. sugar

2 tbsp. olive oil

salt

pepper

Cut meat into strips about 3 1/2 inches wide. Pound these to tenderize and also to thin and widen them. Season with salt, pepper, and garlic while tenderizing. Mix the onion, chayote, and tomatoes in a bowl, adding the bread crumbs, egg, and tomato sauce. Spread this mixture over each piece of meat, which is then rolled and wrapped with a slice of bacon that is held in place with a toothpick. Place these rolls in heated oil in a skillet and brown quickly. Reduce heat to medium, adding lime juice, sugar, and Worcestershire sauce. Simmer until meat is tender, adding more water during the cooking if necessary. Serves 3-4.

Steak Stuffed with Oysters

3 lbs. of steak (round steak is suitable), about ½ inch thick and cut into two equal portions

3 tbsp. flour

1 clove garlic, crushed

¼ tsp. paprika

½ tsp. salt

¼ tsp. pepper

¼ cup water

1 cup oysters, chopped

2 cups bread crumbs

2 stalks celery, diced

1 small onion, diced
4 tbsp. butter or margarine, melted

Depending on cut of steak, tenderize by pounding and sprinkling with tenderizer. Place one piece of steak in baking pan and cover with oyster filling made by mixing lightly the chopped oysters, bread crumbs, diced celery, diced onion, and melted butter. Put other piece of steak on top, sprinkling with flour and adding the seasonings—garlic, paprika, salt, and pepper. Add water to pan and place in oven at 375 degrees for an hour. Serves 3-4.

Note: If single piece of steak is preferred, it can be rolled and skewered after filling is spread over it. Also, vegetables can be added around the steak if desired—potatoes, carrots, onions, cabbage, chayotes—about half an hour after the steak is placed in oven.

Pork and Pineapple

2 lbs. lean pork, diced
1 green pepper, sliced
1 large onion, sliced
1 pineapple, diced
¼ cup pineapple juice
¼ cup water
2 tbsp. brown sugar
2 tbsp. vinegar
1 tsp. salt
1 tbsp. flour
1 tbsp. olive oil

Mix flour, vinegar, sugar, water, salt and ¼ cup pineapple juice. Cook on medium heat, stirring until mixture thickens. Brown pork in olive oil. Pour sauce over the meat and continue cooking on medium-low heat for about half an hour. Add the diced pineapple, onion, and green pepper, cooking for additional 5-8 minutes. Serves 3-4.

West Indian Roast Pork

  4 lb. pork loin
  ¼ cup olive oil or peanut oil
  1 medium green pepper, chopped
  1 medium onion, chopped
  1 clove garlic crushed (or ⅛ tsp. garlic powder)
  1 medium can tomato sauce
  1 tbsp. chili powder
  ½ cups chopped ripe olives
  2 cups cooked rice
  salt
  pepper

Split roast so that stuffing can be put inside. Saute green pepper, onion, and garlic in oil until tender. Add tomato sauce plus 1/2 cup of water. Simmer for a few minutes, then add chili powder. Add chopped olives, then salt and pepper to taste. Continue to simmer for 4 to 5 minutes. Pour about half of this sauce into the rice, then put rice inside the roast. Cook roast for approximately 2 hours in oven preheated to 350 degrees, then remove and add remaining rice and sauce to the roast and around it. Continue cooking for 1 hour. Serves 3-4.

Spareribs and Pineapple

  3 lbs. spareribs, cut apart
  ⅓ cup corn flour
  2 tbsp. black molasses
  ¼ pint cooking oil
  1 can pineapple chunks
  ½ cup sugar
  2 green peppers, diced
  2 cups vinegar

Bring about 5 cups of water to a boil and then stir in 1 cup of vinegar. Add ribs. Bring to a boil again and simmer for about 30 minutes. Drain. Stir the molasses into the sifted corn flour. Brush this mixture onto ribs, then brown the ribs in oil in a skillet. In a deep skillet, mix 1 cup of water with about 1/2 cup of pineapple juice and the remaining vinegar. Add the sugar, heat, and stir until sugar is dissolved. Add spareribs and bring to a boil. Cover tightly and simmer for 30 minutes. Turn ribs several times. Add the pineapple chunks and the green pepper, then simmer for about 5 minutes. Serve while hot. Serves 4-6.

INDEX

Note: For the cook's convenience, we have attempted to make this index very complete, listing each time an ingredient is used. For example, if you happen to have an abundance of a certain "secondary" ingredient on hand, (e.g., celery or onion), you can find many recipes that use them other than those recipes in which they are featured.

Index

Index

If you enjoyed reading this book, here are some other Pineapple Press titles you might enjoy as well. To request our complete catalog or to place an order, write to Pineapple Press, P.O. Box 3889, Sarasota, Florida 34230, or call 1-800-PINEAPL (746-3275). Or visit our website at www.pineapplepress.com.

Essential Catfish Cookbook by Shannon Harper & Janet Cope. Mouth-watering recipes that call for succulent catfish and a variety of easy-to find ingredients. Learn about the private life of the captivating catfish and enjoy this Southern delicacy. ISNB 1-56164-201-0 (pb)

Exotic Foods: A Kitchen & Garden Guide by Marian Van Atta. Grow avocado, mango, carambola, guava, kiwi, pomegranate, and other rare delights in your subtropical backyard. Includes planting and growing instructions as well as over one hundred recipes for enjoying your bountiful crops. ISBN 1-56164-215-0 (pb)

The Everglades: River of Grass, 50th Anniversary Edition by Marjory Stoneman Douglas. This is the treasured classic of nature writing that captured attention all over the world and launched the fight to save the Everglades when it was first published. The 50th Anniversary Edition includes an update on the events in the Glades in the last ten years. ISBN 1-56164-135-9 (hb)

Growing Family Fruit and Nut Trees by Marian Van Atta. What better way to celebrate your family than by growing a tree whose delicious fruit will be a yearly reminder of important events? Learn to choose the right trees and to keep them healthy and bountiful. ISBN 1-56164-001-8 (pb)

Guide to the Gardens of Florida by Lilly Pinkas. Organized by region, this guide provides detailed information on the featured species and facilities offered by Florida's public gardens. Includes 16 pages of color photos and 40 line drawings. ISBN 1-56164-169-3 (pb)

Mastering the Art of Florida Seafood by Lonnie T. Lynch. Includes tips on purchasing, preparing, and serving fish and shellfish—with alligators thrown in for good measure. Includes tips for artistic food placement, food painting techniques, and more. ISBN 1-56164-176-6 (pb)